THE YANOMAMI AND THEIR INTERPRETERS

Fierce People or Fierce Interpreters?

Frank A. Salamone

University Press of America, Inc.
Lanham • New York • Oxford

Copyright © 1997 by
University Press of America,® Inc.
4720 Boston Way
Lanham, Maryland 20706

12 Hid's Copse Rd.
Cummor Hill, Oxford OX2 9JJ

Library of Congress Cataloging-in-Publication Data

Salamone, Frank A.
The Yanomami and their interpreters : fierce people or fierce
interpreters? / Frank A. Salamone.
p.   cm
1. Yanomamo Indians--Social conditions. 2. Yanomamo Indians--
Missions. 3. Yanomamo Indians--Public opinion. 4. Public opinion--
South America. 5. South America--Race relations. I. Title.
F2520.1Y3S25   1997   305.898--dc21   96-49962 CIP

ISBN 0-7618-0654-7 (cloth: alk. ppr.)

Dedication

This book is dedicated to my wife, Virginia, who encouraged me to continue when odds seemed stacked against me. Our children, Frank and Kitty, keep me on target whenever I want to give up. My son, Mark, has given me four wonderful grandchildren and I wish him to know that I admire his own perseverance and appreciate his love. My mother, Frances Salamone, has been my supporter all my life. This book dedication only properly thanks her.

Contents

Preface

This book came about as a result of one of the nastiest disputes in the history of anthropology. The slaughter of the Yanomami by illegal Brazilian miners in 1993 was the immediate cause of Napoleon Chagnon's attack on the Salesian missionaries. Chagnon believed that the Salesians had been keeping him out of the Venezuelan Amazon region for years. When the Bishop of Amazonas, a Salesian missionary, ordered him out of the Amazon, Chagnon erupted and took his case to the popular press. The Salesians replied in kind.

I was pleased to go to the Amazon area for the Salesians to investigate the charges and counter-charges. Thanks to Luisa Margoleis, the director of a research group at the Catholic University in Caracas, I decided to seek to bring the disputants together at the 1994 Annual Meetings of the American Anthropological Association. That they all agreed was a minor miracle.

Since that meeting I have been seeking to put the results on the record. I have added material not presented at the meeting for the sake of clarity. There have been setbacks. Various people have displayed their tempers. However, enough support from scholars has been demonstrated to encourage me to continue with the project. I believe I owe it to the Yanomami to put their plight before students. I found their hospitality and curiosity a delight and hope to return for a longer period.

I hope students will find the book an aid to understanding a much-maligned and mistreated people. Moreover, I hope this book stimulates them to read more about the Yanomami. Many sources are cited and the key arguments presented in this work. They are a fascinating people and have much to offer the world into the next millennium. Certainly, they have become a "representative tribal group," as Chagnon notes. They have focused our attention on the problems of other tribal groups throughout the world.

Finally, I hope the student realizes that the Yanomami are not fierce people. There are aspects of their lives that demand actions that many Yanomami do not like. As they point out, there are aspects in Western culture that are far fiercer than their own. As Cesar Ziminawe states in this work, "I have killed but I am not a killer." Whatever else they have done or failed to do, the missionaries have sought to enable the Yanomami to live in peace and survive into the next century.

This book examines the extent to which missionaries and anthropologists have aided or failed to aid the Yanomami in the hopes that we can all do better as a result of that examination.

Chapter 1

Background to the Battle and Truce

Frank A. Salamone

On December 2, 1994, an extraordinary event took place at the annual meeting of the American Anthropological Association in Atlanta Georgia. Napoleon Chagnon, a renowned anthropologist whose studies of the Yanomami of Venezuela are familiar to all anthropology students in the United States, met with Father Jose Bortoli, a Salesian missionary to the Yanomami on the Orinoco River for 20 years. Chagnon's feud with the Salesians had been raging for some time. Mutually incriminating charges had surfaced in the <u>New York Times</u> and the *Chronicle of Higher Education.*

The triggering event in this feud was the slaughter of 16 or 17 Yanomami in 1993 by illegal Brazilian miners. Chagnon and his friend Charles Brewer Carias had gone into the area to investigate the event. Their Presidential appointment was superseded and another Presidential commission named. The circumstances surrounding these appointments are still a matter of dispute. The Bishop of Amazonas, a member of the commission, ordered Chagnon from the area. Since then the Bishop has been named Archbishop of Caracas.

Chagnon and Bortoli, who are old friends, had a peace meeting in the rain forest at this time at which, Chagnon says, a truce was reached. Chagnon charges that the Salesian missionaries broke their promises to him of a truce by stirring up the Yanomami against him, thereby endangering his life. The Salesians argue that Chagnon and Brewer Carias were engaged in illegal mining themselves and wanted to keep the Yanomami in a kind of human zoo. This zoo-like preserve would retard their technological development, a development many Yanomami themselves say they desire. Of course, that is the nub of the argument between the Salesians and Chagnon; namely, "Who Speaks for the Yanomami?" Chagnon argues that it is only "mission Yanomami" and those controlled by miners who wish technological development. The charges became increasingly bitter and little purpose seemed served by the feud. Nationalistic issues, moreover, became intertwined with theoretical, ethical, and professional ones.

Theoretical issues revolve around the question of the best manner in which to aid indigenous people in meeting the challenges of modernization while retaining their "authenticity." No one seriously doubts that modernization will come. The only doubt is in its impact on local peoples. Moreover, the manner in which local peoples contribute to the planning process, choose their destinies, and prepare for change involve serious ethical issues. These issues touch on matters of hegemony, authenticity, and representativeness. In other words, "Who Speaks for the Yanomami?"

Certainly, older conceptions of uniform cultural units have long passed in the waste bin of discarded colonial ideas. Those who think they know what's best for the Yanomami, whether anthropologists or missionaries, presume to speak for the Yanomami even while denying that they do so. Some are honest enough to note that they are doing so only for a, usually indeterminate, period of time. That time is generally stated as "until the Yanomami can speak for themselves" or "until some representative method of Yanomami government is formed by the Yanomami."

This approach raises the ugly issue of paternalism, an issue that is addressed in each of the separate presentations. It, of course, must be weighed against the issue of Yanomami survival which missionaries and anthropologists agree depends to a great extent upon ensuring world-wide attention to their plight. Thus, a delicate ethical issue has become part of the debate; namely, how can people help the Yanomami without making them dependent.

In addition to the difficulties centering on Yanomami involvement in planning their own destiny, there is the problem of intellectual imperialism. Simply put, anthropology is an international discipline. However, anthropologists from smaller nations often feel that American scholars often act as if they own rights to the study of indigenous peoples. Some Venezuelan anthropologists, for example, resented Chagnon's work with the Yanomami and believed he was trespassing on their preserve. Others were more open to his work but believed he was engaged in political issues that Americans should avoid. Much heat and only a little light was generated by the dispute.

As I explain in my chapter, I became involved in the dispute because of my previous success in working with missionaries in Africa. I neither praise nor condemn missionaries out of hand but, rather, attempt to assess their actions as I do any other people whom I study. My field of expertise has been African religion and ethnicity, particularly in Nigeria. Along the way, I have focused on the role missionaries play in these processes and, logically, on missionary culture itself. I have generally earned a reputation for fairness from missionaries while attempting to remain honest to the empirical reality and my interpretation of it.

Therefore, I was quite interested in the dispute that arose between Napoleon Chagnon and the Salesian missionaries in 1993 and which came to a boiling point in 1994. The dispute threatened to embarrass both anthropology and the missionaries while overshadowing the very real plight of the Yanomami. I followed the charges and counter charges rather closely, and when Father Edward Cappelletti, the director of the Salesian missions, wrote a letter to the *Anthropology Newsletter* presenting the Salesian side of the dispute with Chagnon, I decided to call him and seek a meeting. Since we are both located in New Rochelle, New York, that was an easy matter to arrange.

In May 1994, we ate at a fine Italian restaurant, La Riserva, and the talk was easy and pleasant. I learned a bit about the Salesian work in the Amazon. When I casually remarked that it would be good to have a neutral anthropologist investigate the charges and counter charges, Cappelletti coolly asked why I could not be that person. I explained my lack of knowledge about the Yanomami, the Amazon, and Venezuela - not to mention my lack of funds. He replied that none of these mattered. He would pay my way and I could learn about the rest before my trip!

I do find some broader theoretical issues in mission activities just as I do in those of anthropologists or colonial administrators. Each of these groups consists of expatriates who are change agents and who must learn something of the culture, society, and people they seek, directly or indirectly, to change. They set up separate residences and never truly can become "natives" in the groups among which they work. At the same time, I have a critical but passionate love for anthropology and academic freedom.

I told Cappelletti that while I generally get on well with missionaries, we have had our theoretical differences and ethical differences as my articles and books have demonstrated. I have been open in my skepticism regarding the success of mission work, while remaining a practicing Catholic after my fashion. As a fellow Italian-American, Cappelletti smiled his understanding and stated that he was willing to take his chances with me. On those terms, I accepted his offer to investigate, at Salesian expense, the issues involved in the Chagnon-Salesian dispute.

I spent the next six months preparing for the brief ten day trip. I spoke to various people about the issues at stake, read as much as I could given my five class schedule at Iona, studied Italian to speak to the Italian Salesians, and wondered at my sanity in undertaking the research. After all, I knew little about the ethnological situation there, had never been to South America, and was putting myself in the middle of a volatile situation that required diplomatic skills that I was not certain I possess. In sum, I was exposing myself to possible hostile criticism. Nevertheless, because I believed in the importance of the issues involved, and because I refuse to appear cowardly, I decided to do the best I could.

After making many calls to Venezuela and receiving Luisa Margolies's aid in contacting people, in November 1994 I traveled to Caracas and the Amazon rain forest and spoke with Salesian missionaries, a human rights lawyer, Venezuelan and other anthropologists, Venezuelan doctors, and the Yanomami. I spoke with anyone, in fact, who was available and who had any information concerning the issues involved.

Upon returning to the United States, I spoke with Napoleon Chagnon. At Luisa Margolies's urging, I invited him to meet with

Padre Bortoli at a session of the American Anthropological Association meetings I had scheduled on Anthropology and Theology. I also conveyed Luisa Margolies's personal invitation to meet with her session on the state of Indians in Venezuela. Margolies is the director of Venezuela's anthropological research center. Chagnon graciously accepted these invitations and arranged his schedule in order to participate in the meetings. Padre Bortoli had also agreed to attend the meetings and discuss his differences with Chagnon.

On the evening before the meeting, Bortoli, Chagnon, Dr. Teo Marcano, Father Donald Delaney, and I met for dinner to discuss the issues and the procedure for the program. Delaney is a Salesian who accompanied me to the Amazon and works in the Salesian mission headquarters in New Rochelle, New York. Marcano is a Venezuelan doctor who has worked with the Salesians and Chagnon. It was obvious to me that Bortoli and Chagnon were old friends who were quite fond of each other.

That cordiality carried over into their public meeting the next day. Plans were laid for cooperative research and the easing of Chagnon's difficulties in obtaining travel permits for entrance into the Venezuelan rain forest. Their meetings and public statements mapped out their common concerns for the Yanomami as well as their publicly stated wishes for joint medical, anthropological, and missionary endeavors to aid the Yanomami. The general tenor of the transcripts of that meeting is that not only had a truce been reached but that the truce would lead to a new era of peaceful cooperation. Each party involved believed that their truce would further the interests of the Yanomami. The problem is that each party viewed these interests in a somewhat different fashion. Each also spoke with different Yanomami and interpreted their responses in contrasting manners.

Because of the importance of this public exchange of honest opinions, I had the tapes of the session transcribed in hope of having the record available for professionals and students. I sent these transcripts to the principals involved for their comments and corrections. Additionally, at Chagnon's suggestion, I contacted Greg Sanford of the New Tribes Mission and received total cooperation from him. I received help in this effort from Tom Headland of the Summer Institute of Linguistics. Contrary to their undeserved reputation, the New Tribes missionaries proved easy to work with and were eager to tell their own story. I assured them I would make no substantive changes in their chapter and have not done so. They also supplied photos portraying the Yanomami in more realistic light than most ethnographies. Comments from the Yanomami who reside near the Salesian and New Tribes stations were gathered at the suggestion of Wadsworth press editors and Susan Skomal, media relations editor of the American Anthropological Association. I solicited statements from Yanomami regarding their views of anthropologists and missionaries. These are presented here in translation, usually from Spanish and sometimes from Yanomami. I have presented their views in a chapter, identifying the source of quotes and paraphrases where appropriate.

After all, the Yanomami should speak for the Yanomami. Moreover, it is essential to provide at least the flavor of Yanomami discourse and the wide variety of opinions that exist within Yanomami society. It is one thing to state simplistically that Yanomami should speak for the Yanomami. It is another to realize that there is not a single Yanomami opinion on any significant issue and that Yanomami differ among themselves depending on their location, contacts, and personal stake in any particular issue. They are articulate and know what they want regardless of what well-meaning outsiders may think.

True human respect is about the ability to air our differences openly and still remain friends. I have great respect for all participants in this volume and deep love for the Yanomami whom I just barely met and with whom I hope to become better acquainted in the future. They, after all, should be the focus of our attention, for both anthropology and missionization exist only so long as we keep their welfare and that of other marginalized peoples in mind. In the truest sense, we exist for them and not they for us.

Since the meetings, the Salesians have failed to proceed with an agreement to work on a joint demographic research endeavor. Moreover, Brother Jon Finkers has published one or two articles attacking Chagnon. Chagnon, on the other hand, has refrained from resuming public attacks on the Salesians, still hoping that peace will last and lead to fruitful research. Personally, I have tried to explain the intricacies of the issues and their deeper implications for anthropology and missiology. For example, there is a basic similarity between members of each group. Members of each group are filled with a strong sense of mission and a desire to learn what is best for "their" people. Over time, committed members of each profession cannot help but learn indigenous categories of thought which alter their own perception of reality and the meaning of their own native systems. Furthermore, they realize that unless they learn to translate the world into indigenous categories of reality, they cannot truly communicate with "their" people.

Many anthropologists have learned that missionaries provide a quick access to these categories and to indigenous people who can teach them how to tap these resources. Many missionaries, in turn, have learned that anthropologists provide analytical and theoretical tools that enable them to make sense of their surroundings in ways that have proved hitherto almost impossible. These methodological and theoretical vehicles, moreover, have served as midwives in the radicalization of missionaries in Latin America and Africa through providing them a relativizing and sensitizing perspective on "reality," one more in conformity with those whom they have come to serve.

Joint efforts of missionaries and anthropologists, moreover, have been valuable in preserving the Yanomami from extinction. These efforts have made the Yanomami famous. Their "fame" has been a valuable weapon in Yanomami self-preservation against the inroads of threats from modernization; such as the influx of illegal gold miners and development schemes that would destroy the ecological basis of their lives.

There are approximately 22,500 Yanomami in the Amazon Basin, making them the largest indigenous group in the Amazon Basin. These Indians are spread among roughly 225 villages in Venezuela and Brazil in an area in the Amazon rain forest to the north of the Amazon River. Each Yanomami village is autonomous and has alliances with other villages. These villages carry on warfare with other villages periodically. There have been bitter disputes regarding just how frequently these clashes occur.

Clashes with outsiders have led to noisy arguments within anthropology in particular and in development circles in general regarding the best ways in which to safeguard the Yanomami. At times, it appeared that the interests or desires of the Yanomami themselves were being overlooked as one faction or another attacked the position of their opponents. Each faction purported to speak for the Yanomami. As I write these words, the worst flood in their recorded history has hit the Yanomami area, adding further to their woes. The Yanomami have asked that people stop coming tho their area in expensive helicopters and planes and send them real aid.

Therefore, I have urged people concerned with the issues to write fairly about them and to refrain from inciting the parties to resume their bickering. Both Chagnon and the Salesians have performed important services in preserving the Yanomami. It is foolhardy to incite a resumption of their dispute. Bortoli and Chagnon are aware of this fact and wish to advance the interests of the Yanomami as they see fit. There is room for honest disagreement in their interpretations. The Yanomami themselves are producing various spokespeople who represent different interests within their society. The situation will become complex enough without seeking to create further furor that will aid no one's true interests but only provide an academic sideshow.

In an attempt to work toward peace, I present the documents presented here. They stand as a record of what took place on December 2, 1994, in Atlanta, Georgia. Since then the tenuous peace has more or less held. As with many truces, however, the longed for "peace dividend" has not yet been declared. For the sake of the Yanomami, I hope that dividend comes soon.

Chapter 2

Theoretical Reflections on the Chagnon-Salesian Controversy

Frank A. Salamone

Introduction

Missionary scholars such as Burridge (1991), Donovan (1983), Hillman (1993, 1975, 1965), Kirwin (1987,1988a, 1988b), van der Geest and Kirby (1992), and Whiteman (1985), have long challenged interpretations of Christianity based on Western ideas. Their work has highlighted the problem of adapting Western European Christianity for people whose cultures include theological systems based on concepts different from and even hostile to those of Western thought.

Anthropologists, also, have been struggling to reconcile their discipline's assumptions with the dilemmas and challenges that the basic assumptions of Western thought that underlie their field of study may not be so universal as once assumed. This challenge has served to upset a number of anthropologists who feel that their very reason for being has been called into question. I argue that in situations already loaded with anxiety, such as fieldwork, challenges to old ideas only sharpen conditions of confusion which often lead to violent outbursts against those whose world-system is perceived as a threatening challenge to one's own.

The missionary-anthropologist relationship, in this perspective, is but a structural variety of a more basic relationship; specifically, a relationship between those who reside in a community in order to transform it according to some higher authority, termed "God," and those who seek to obtain knowledge in the name of another higher authority, termed "science." Since the missionary is often on the scene long before the anthropologist, he or she often possesses resources essential to the successful completion of many anthropological studies; for example, knowledge of the geography, understanding of local power structures, ties to officials, and access to indigenous peoples. Whenever pragmatism demands cooperation, hostility will normally be repressed. In a complementary fashion, however, whenever an anthropologist perceives that a missionary is obstructing successful completion of a project, overt hostility will erupt. At best, the missionary-anthropologist relationship is one charged with uncertainty, for both share a number of professional and personality traits and it is often their underlying similarities rather than their differences that result in conflict. Both, for example, ideally share a commitment to the welfare of indigenous peoples, according to their lights, and both also have an irrepressible streak of romanticism that dooms them to being forever marginal to their own cultures and societies, never fully at home anywhere and always seeking to be at home somewhere else.

It is a truism that people of good will can, and often do, disagree. Similarly, it is also a truism that love and hate are but two sides of the same coin, that love is inherently an ambivalent relationship. The history of anthropology, in fact, is marked by often violent disagreements. Foremost among these clashes have been those between missionaries and anthropologists. Often that disagreement stems from intense concern for the welfare of indigenous peoples and the best way to promote that welfare. It is important, therefore, that the disputes concerning indigenous interests not shift from the native peoples themselves, but always keep the native peoples in focus. It is also important, though a subsidiary issue, that partisans disagree without being disagreeable.

It is, therefore, commendable that both Napoleon Chagnon and Jose Bortoli agreed to discuss the issues that divided them over the past year or so.[1] This disagreement placed the Yanomami and their plight squarely in the center of discussion and such a discussion offers the best opportunity to air controversial and significant issues of interest. Certainly these are of interest to missiology and anthropology, but they are a far greater concern to both discipline's stated goals of serving the interest of the peoples among whom anthropologists and missionaries alike profess to serve.

The recent dispute, now thankfully laid to rest, between Napoleon Chagnon and the Salesian Fathers, provides a significant case study of a major dispute involving missionaries and anthropologists (For example, Chagnon 1993 and 1994). I became involved in the dispute as a result of my long-time research into the cultures of missionaries and anthropologists as these affected the field situation of ethnographers. Additionally, over time, I extended my research into missionary cultures and their impact on the culture and behavior of indigenous societies.

The Salesian Fathers asked me to go to Venezuela to look into the increasingly bitter dispute between Chagnon and the Salesian missionaries. I alerted Father Edward Cappelletti to the fact that I, also, had been involved in differences with Catholic missionaries during the course of my own field work in Nigeria. While it is true that our differences have generally been patched up and my overall association with missionaries has been cordial, still we do not agree on all issues. The Salesians assured me of a free hand in reporting my findings. They guaranteed me total access to their stations and to the Yanomami who resided near those stations on the Orinoco.

What I discovered was, to a large extent, what I had anticipated. People of good will had allowed themselves to be pushed into positions they felt uncomfortable occupying. Certainly, there were, and are, very real differences between Chagnon and the Salesians. These differences, however, had never seriously interfered with their cooperation over their long mutual history stretching back into the 1960s, an association that saw them cooperate in a friendly fashion on a number of projects (for example, Chagnon, Bortoli, and Eguillor 1988).

The authentic question, then, lay in what really lurked behind the explosive events of 1993-94. There were, of course, very serious issues involved in the dispute that had lain festering for years. The roots of the dispute lay in events of 1989-90. However, the Yanomami massacre in August 1993 at Hashimo-thieri provided the occasion for an explosion of invective between the two sides. It is essential to inquire just why this human tragedy involving Yanomami led to a missionary-anthropologist confrontation.

There were two Presidential Commissions chosen to investigate the massacre, one with Chagnon and one with Bishop Ignacio Velasco. The clash between these two competing Presidential Commissions, was an embarrassment to Chagnon. Most anthropologists, including me, instinctively flocked to Chagnon's side when they heard that Bishop Ignacio Velasco ordered an anthropologist from his field site. Further reflection and developments, however, led many to suspend final judgement pending additional investigation.[2]

As Cardozo notes:

As I understand events, Velasco never ordered anybody out of Parima. He doesn't have that authority. It was the designated 'fiscal' from the Fiscalia General de la Republica who did so (E-mail May 16, 1995).

Most American anthropologists, however, did not discover that fact until much later in the dispute.

The Issues

A number of key issues appear to underlie the dispute between the Salesians and Chagnon. Principal among these concerns is control of research in the Orinoco region of Venezuela. The issue, in many people's views, is whether Chagnon or the Salesians should control research in the sector. Chagnon's statements imply that he would either exclude Salesians from the area or allow them in only if they subject their work to his evaluation.

From this perspective, the entire issue resolves itself into a "Turf War" and the Salesians simply joined with other enemies of Chagnon in a united front. Prominent in this phalanx was the French anthropologist, Jacques Lizot. Lizot and Chagnon have often differed bitterly on theoretical and substantive issues. In addition, a number of Venezuelan anthropologists resent what they perceive, rightly or not, as Chagnon's efforts to establish American research control over a region in their country.

Chagnon himself has clearly stated the issue:

> ... the central issue regarding the future of the Yanomamo: what do informed and concerned citizens think should be the respective roles and authorities of (1) the Venezuelan and Brazilian governments, (2) religious institutions such as the several Mission groups working among the Yanomamo, (3) NGOs, (4) medical researchers and practitioners, and (5) scientific researchers from many different disciplines? All the above now play some role in this process, but the roles are poorly defined and who has what kinds of authority is an open question that, if unresolved, will lead to increasing chaos and increasing peril for the Yanomamo. How should all of these groups, ideally, interact and cooperate with each other? ... Whatever exists on paper or in theory, an outside observer would be obliged to conclude that in Venezuela the de facto authority determining the future of the Venezuelan Yanomamo rests in the hands of the Salesian Missions of Amazonas. Given the importance of this to the future of the Yanomamo, this apparent abrogation of legal authority and responsibility by the Venezuelan government is something to which serious thought be given and should be widely discussed in Venezuela (1994 Jul-Aug:161-162). <Translation from Spanish by Napoleon Chagnon>

Chagnon's original research, however, was carried out near a settled mission area, that of the New Tribes Mission. Not surprisingly, many missionaries perceived this attack as a betrayal of their hospitality. Although the primary research for Chagnon's "the fierce people" was not conducted primarily at the Salesian stations, the Salesians have aided Chagnon and other anthropologists from their coming to the Orinoco in the mid-1950s.

Moreover, although the story of *Yanomamo: The Fierce People* is familiar to most basic anthropology students, the Salesians are upset that most students do not, however, get to know that events are more complicated than they might appear. The situation described in the book is not, as students might infer, an everyday one.[3] Missionaries have been quick to indicate that Chagnon's description of the Yanomami has not been an accurate one (Finkers 1994, for example). They have been joined by others whom Chagnon once deemed his friends (Asch 1991, for example, and Good 1992, his former student).

Chagnon, himself, at that time and others often was a man under extreme pressure. After all, although Chagnon was the anthropologist who had "opened up" Yanomami research, nonetheless he was out of the Yanomami area from the late 1970s until 1985. Therefore, he sought a means to stabilize his position and assure himself of research access. He concocted a biosphere project with Charles Brewer Carias, a Venezuelan dentist, who had political connections. This scheme would enable him to maintain great control of projects in the Venezuelan Yanomami territory. Unfortunately, Brewer Carias is not a favorite of either Venezuela's anthropological or mission community and this tie did little to heal the rift between Chagnon and members of these Venezuelan communities.[4]

Chagnon blames much of his problems regarding access to research on the Salesian missionaries. Although he had indeed collaborated on projects with the Salesians, he nonetheless regarded them as obstacles to his free admittance to the Amazon area. The biosphere would be closed to all but productive research. As senior anthropologist and director of the biosphere, Chagnon, a proven anthropologist, would decide which research would be in the Yanomami's interest. It would also ensure him access to the Yanomami.

Terence Turner, however, offers a somewhat differing anthropological interpretation of the situation.[5] Turner agrees that Chagnon indeed raises serious issues regarding development, issues of concern to people of good will, missionaries and anthropologists alike. Chagnon raises a significant concern regarding whether the higher death rate at Salesian missions communities is a result of long-term Yanomami settlement having a damaging effect on Yanomami nutrition through their over hunting's leading to resource exhaustion.[6] Chagnon accused the Salesians, in sum, of killing the Yanomami with kindness at their frontier posts. Turner, however, questions this conclusion, asking "Is it that their posts are collecting points for the desperately ill or that Salesian policies are bad?" In short, he argues that it is essential to ascertain the cause of the high death rate at Salesian posts.

In fact, Turner provides the strongest statement on record of any American anthropological opposition to Chagnon. He accuses him of "unconscionable slandering of those helping the Yanomami," "a sociopath who slanders those who help the Yanomami without regard to the Yanomami themselves." Turner views Chagnon as "a liar whose lies damage the Yanomami." Among Turner's specific complaints is the fact that Chagnon's labeling of the Yanomami as somehow inherently "fierce" is still quoted in the Brazilian press in anti-Yanomami articles. While admitting that a person's scientific writing is often distorted in the popular press, Turner point out that Chagnon has never repudiated the uses made of his work. In fairness to Chagnon, it must be noted that he does, in fact, repudiate this misuse in his 1983 version of *Yanomamo: The Fierce People* (Chagnon 1983: 213-214).

Turner repeated many of his charges in a question to Chagnon at the meetings of the American Anthropological Association in Atlanta, Georgia, on December 2, 1994, at the Session on Anthropology and Theology. Since the question sums up many of the charges against Chagnon, I reproduce the transcript here of the question and of Chagnon's response.[7]

I have two questions, the first about the problem of who speaks for the Yanomami, the Yanomami leadership, with particular emphasis on the case of Davi Kopinawa. Professor Chagnon has just said some kind words about Davi so he's obviously a nice guy and means well. And I think that's true. He also said that he seems to have all his remarks scripted for him. What he says isn't his own; it doesn't come out of his own mouth or at least his own heart. It comes from Anglos, I suppose. This is not true. I speak as someone who is listed as a co-author of the longest printed text that Davi Kopinawa is down in. That's a text printed in full in *Cultural Survival*. It has an article which I suggest you all look at, if you're interested, called "I Fight Because I Am Alive." Now this article, which was partly reprinted in the newsletter of this association, was dictated to me by Davi. I asked the questions, what I hoped were leading questions to get him to address points that were issued between the Yanomami of Brazil and the government of Brazil about the whole problem of the reserve that was then in question. Davi answered these questions at great length and in terms which I certainly could never have invented. They are terms which are soaked with Yanomami concepts, Yanomami cosmology, Yanomami ideas of diseases, Yanomami ideas of cosmic order and disorder. These are not concepts which were supplied by me or by anyone else to Davi. But Davi has used this rhetoric on other occasions. He has also used the rhetoric of conservationist organizations. He is trying to represent his idea of the interest of his people in terms that we can understand that will be real for us. He's trying to manipulate our rhetoric but, or hence, which I think he sincerely believes are the ends of his people. He is not a mouthpiece for anybody. Now Professor Chagnon has recently said in print in the American Anthropological Association newsletter that I have forfeited all credibility as an anthropologist because I have referred to Davi Kopinawa as a genuine Yanomami leader, whereas he is only a mouthpiece for NGOs. It's not only a matter of this being false, it's a matter of this undermining the most effective spokesman for Yanomami interests, although it's quite correct to say that Davi is not a chief of all the Yanomami, he's only a leader of one section of the Yanomami, but nevertheless, he is the most effective spokesman for many of the general interests of the Yanomami to the outside world. He is someone who has made a political difference for the Yanomami, especially in Brazil. To undermine him in such an untruthful way, without knowing him and obviously without taking the trouble to analyze the text of his speeches of his publications, directly damages the interest of the Yanomami. And I submit that this is in apparent contradiction to the ethical dictates of this association in which the rules of professional responsibility which hold above all that we as anthropologists should endeavor not to damage the interest of the people we work with. Their interests must come first unless it's a matter of declaring scientific truth which is not the issue in the case.

SALAMONE: Napoleon, would you like to ...

CHAGNON: You're goddman right I'd like to. I came here in a spirit of conciliation with an interest in advocating the rights of the Yanomami and I'm going to ignore all of Professor Turner's comments, which I think are out of place in the spirit of what we're attempting to accomplish in this meeting today.

The spirit to which Chagnon refers is the spirit of reconciliation which took place publicly at the session on Anthropology and Theology at which he and the Salesian representative, Jose Bortoli, agreed to a truce.

On their part, the Salesians in New Rochelle have stirred up controversy and animosity regarding their mailing of anonymous articles. There were two distinct distributions of material. One went to anthropologists listed in the AAA Guide to Departments. The other was placed on a table at the American Anthropological Association Annual Meetings. There are various people who might have translated and distributed the Venezuelan articles. No one is, however, willing to go on record claiming or naming these people. Some think that a disgruntled former student of Chagnon sent them. Other Venezuelan anthropologists, however, suggested that Bishop Velasco sent the clippings and then the Salesians sent a mailing out to people on the American Anthropological Association's mailing list. The clippings, sent by Velasco, were translated, either by a Salesian translator or by one of Chagnon's anthropological opponents. Additionally, it is beyond dispute that the Salesians carried a package of materials to the 1993 American Anthropological Association meetings in Washington, DC, leaving this package on a display table with no identification as to their origin. Unfortunately, the Salesians still do not understand the anger most anthropologists feel regarding the receipt of anonymous mailings and handouts.

I asked Father Cappelletti why he did not understand that anger. His response was that the articles enclosed in the package were from reputable sources and those articles were clearly identified. The fact that anthropologists are plagued throughout the year with anonymous mailings from religious sources damning us for embracing the evils of evolution or some other heresy meant nothing to him. Nor did the fact that American academics still remember the evils of McCarthyism and its hidden accusers. Certainly, the subtleties of subjective selectivity in article selection did not impress him. There was no argument I could put forth that moved him to consider how repugnant anonymous accusations were to American academics.

The Salesians argue, moreover, that their action was in response to an Op Ed article Chagnon (1993) published in the New York Times, essentially charging the Salesians with inciting the Yanomami to murder him. Additionally, Chagnon attacked the Salesians for selling rifles to their mission Yanomami which these Yanomami used to kill other Yanomami in warfare. Moreover, Chagnon charged that the Salesians had distorted the Yanomami's way of life and were responsible for bringing epidemics into their area. In sum, the article, intentionally or not, was a rehearsal of most of the charges anthropologists had hurled at missionaries over the years.[8]

The Salesians responded in kind. Their mailing and distribution campaign was but part of a concerted effort to discredit Chagnon. They worked with Jacques Lizot who launched a bitter attack on Chagnon.[9] Other attacks followed, most notably that of Timothy Asch.[10] Brother Finkers, a Salesian brother whom Chagnon accused of not rendering medical aid to the Yanomami in an emergency, responded in an article.[11] Some attacks were less open and conducted by people who refuse to go on the record, some in fear of retaliation and others for less noble reasons.

In any case, the Salesians were not "a small minor Italian order" who would take a frontal attack quietly.[12] They enlisted their vast network in support of their efforts and were prepared to escalate their efforts if they saw a need to do so.[13] The Salesians were frustrated with their failure to obtain Op Ed space in the New York Times and the refusal of *Science* and other journals to print material on the Yanomami that contradicted Chagnon's position.

In the midst of this furor, the major issues were often lost, misplaced, and redefined according to the interests of those listing the issues. The underlying point, according to Jesus Cardozo, is how well Chagnon gets along with the Yanomami. In essence, Cardozo sees three discrete issues in the dispute: Chagnon and the Yanomami; Chagnon's accusations; and Chagnon's personality. In common with most other anthropologists, he argues that Chagnon's embrace of the theory of sociobiology be disregarded. After all, Cardozo, himself, is interested in sociobiology and Chagnon's student but disagrees with him regarding his evaluation of the Salesians. He states that Chagnon is opportunistic, noting that his charges appear in the New York Times, the *Times Literary Supplement*, *The Chronicle of Higher Education* and other such popular journals. All of these articles, however, according to Cardozo, ignore the fact that he was illegally in the area.[14]

Luisa Margolies, who with her husband Graziano Gasparini collaborated with Chagnon from 1986-1989, notes that it is ironic to see Chagnon cast as a victim after his attacks. In fact, Cardozo and Margolies counseled that only by focusing on the attacks could any sense by made of the imbroglio. Indeed, there are facts that help explain the attacks.[15]

First, there have been significant changes in Salesian mission organization. Prominently, there is currently a policy of concentrated planning in distinction to the pre-1976 policy of independent stations. The Salesians, under the influence of Jacques Lizot, have pursued a policy encouraging non-dependent development among the Yanomami. They have advocated a course in which the Yanomami participate in the planning, development, and control of any schemes in their area. The Salesians, in sum, counsel the Yanomami to pursue only those projects that fall into the category of sustainable development. Moreover, the Salesians have warned the Yanomami about the sources and dangers of epidemics. Consequently, the Yanomami have asked to see the permits of any people entering Amazonas because illegal visitors may be carriers of disease or endanger life as do the illegal miners from Brazil, *garampieros*.

These changes have led to modification in relationships between Chagnon and the Yanomami. Perhaps, the most glaring example is a Yanomami letter sent to a government minister asking that Chagnon be kept out of the area. Chagnon blames the Salesians for encouraging the Yanomami to become aggressive enough to write a letter. Cesar Zimanawe, a Yanomami, states that he wrote the letter unaided and not encouraged by anyone else, including the Salesians. The Salesians, however, did publish the letter in La Iglesia en Amazonas, their Venezuelan organ (1990:20). Since the letter has led to considerable strife, I reproduce it here.

Mavaquite 7-2-90

Senor Chagnon

Nosotros los de Mavaquita, Washere y Quetipapirei theri y Mishi mishitheri no queremos que Usted venga alto Orinoco.

Porque Usted tenia pleito con Washere y ademas no queremos que Saco en Taritatheri Washewetheri Meishi mishither tierre mucha pelic y sangranto mucho los yanomami en la pelicula asi me contos un amigo.

No queremos que saque meas pelicula.

Cesar Ziminawe

(Mister Chagnon,

We of the Mavaquita, Washere and Quetipapirei and Meishi lands don't want you to come to the Alto Orinoco because you fought in the Washere and with their allies and, moreover, we don't want you to take so many pictures and blood samples from so many of the Yanomami. You have taken too many pictures of the Yanomami of Washere and Meishi, taking blood samples as well. As I count you as a friend we expect you to heed our request and stay away.

We don't want you to take any more pictures.

Cesar Ziminawa - Translated by Walter R. Adams)

When I personally questioned Cesar Ziminawe, he maintained that he alone had written the letter. He then launched into an attack on those who believe that Yanomami should remain frozen in time so that anthropologists and other Westerners could come to visit them and admire their primitiveness.

"They come here," he stated, "and take their clothes off so that they can be like us. But if we put clothes on to be like them, they object that we are not authentic. I told Shaki[16] that when he first came here he had an old boat with an old motor. His boats got better as time passed. Then he came in helicopters. I asked him why he could improve and we could not? Why must we paddle in old canoes when we can get motors for our boats?"

Chagnon's depiction of them as fierce people has been an essential part of Yanomami resentment of Chagnon. They argue that although there is violence in their society, they are not violent people. As Cesar Ziminawe told me:

I have killed but I am not a killer. I do not like violence. That is why I am now living near the mission station. It is peaceful here and raids are less likely. No man likes to die. It may be necessary to kill and die but I want to live in peace and be with my children. The missionaries always tell us to be peaceful and to settle our problems through discussion.

This comment came in response to my asking him whether the missionaries had sent him to kill Chagnon as he has charged. After laughing at the thought, he said he did not want to kill Shaki (Bee), the missionaries would never ask any Yanomami to kill anyone else.

Moreover, he asked, "Why doesn't Shaki come and make these charges to my face? That is the Yanomami way."[17]

Cardozo was at a meeting with the Director of Asuntos Indigenas who told him that Chagnon's permit was suspended as a result of Cesar's letter. According to Cardozo, Bortoli advised Chagnon to go to the Orinoco and discuss his problem face-to-face with the Yanomami. He failed to do so. In addition, the minister and other Venezuelans, including Yanomami, charge that Chagnon has neglected to donate promised materials. For example, at the end of his 1985-87 fieldwork he did not donate his outboard motor, dugout canoe, and other materials to the Universidad Central de Venezuela as pledged.

Chagnon, of course, has his own reasons for being angry. Beginning in 1985, according to Cardozo, he has claimed that Yanomami films have been distributed that contain pornography inserted in the middle. These films have been shown in the Shabono. Chagnon feels that their was a conspiracy to undermine his integrity. Cardozo, however, does not believe that the Salesians are responsible for this conspiracy.

> In 1985, during my first visit to the Upper Orinoco, in the village of Hauyapiwei, Chagnon said to me that the Yanomami had complained to him about his taking pictures of them because they had been shown a film made by him that showed naked women's vaginas. Chagnon was angry and ranted about who could have spliced pornographic footage into 'one of his films' (presumably those done by Timothy Asch) and shown to the Yanomami. These are the facts as I know them. I have NEVER heard of any other information that confirmed or even made reference to the existence of such a film not to its alleged exhibition in a shabono or elsewhere. In fact, whenever I have asked Yanomami and missionaries alike in the Upper Orinoco and anthropologists in Caracas, I have always been answered with incredulous laughter at what people perceive as another one of Chagnon's tales. As far as I know, NOBODY has ever heard or seen this film, nor does anyone think it likely that such a film was ever doctored as alleged by Chagnon and then transported with generator, projector, screen and other implements to be shown in a shabono (Cardozo 1995).

On the other hand, however, the Yanomami say that they have seen Chagnon's films, complete with "vaginas," shown in the North. The Yanomami say that other Venezuelans remark that the Yanomami are "just like monkeys." On principle, they object to having their way of life ridiculed and some Yanomami believe that Chagnon's depictions have led to ridicule among their compatriots as well as among people in other countries. In addition, the Yanomami say that he takes too many pictures "is always talking about the dead." In a typically Yanomami aside, however, one of the Yanomami told me, "besides he does not pay us enough for talking about the dead!"

Chagnon believes that the Salesians had pushed the Yanomami into writing the letter. Whether they did or not, it is indisputably true that when Chagnon failed to respond to the letter, which the missionaries delivered to him. They then encouraged the Yanomami to deliver it to the Directora de Asuntos Indigenas to make her aware of the Yanomami's position. They also published that letter in their journal *La Iglesia en Amazonas*. Therefore, when Chagnon wanted to return to the High Orinoco, he was told that there was a problem and that he had to clear that problem before he could carry out any further research. Bortoli, a Salesian missionary, believes that incident was the start of the fighting and confrontation between the Salesians and Chagnon. In this he is in perfect agreement with Chagnon. That confrontation has had some amusing twists.

Interestingly, for example, Chagnon has stated that the Yanomami who speak Spanish are not really authentic Yanomami. That is a charge to which the Yanomami object rather vehemently. They are changing, and it is, truly, the mission that has brought about many changes. However, it is rather naive for any anthropologist to believe that without the mission station the Yanomami would not have changed at all. The real question is whether the manner in which the missionaries have brought about change is compatible with Yanomami culture. Bortoli, in fact, is a great proponent of the process of "inculturation," not to be confused with "enculturation." Nzomiwu"s (1988: 13) sees inculturation as a process related to indigenization.[18]

For Christian theologians it is an incarnational attempt to articulate
the Christian faith clearly in the thought-forms of the environment
in which Christians find themselves but it is not to use such
thought-patterns to introduce ideas which change the meaning and
substance of the Christian message <lower case 'c' in the
original>.

It is simply wrong-headed to state that only those Yanomami
who live in the forest are authentic Yanomami. Such a static and
monolithic view of culture has been long superseded in anthropology and missiology. The Salesians believe that if people
themselves want to change, then outsiders telling them they cannot
change are as guilty of cultural imperialism as those who tell them
how to change. "In other words," as Bortoli states, "if people want
to change, who are we to tell them not to change?"

If the Yanomami are to survive, they must be able to make their
own case in front of Venezuelan officials. The days are passing, the
Salesians believe, when a few machetes will be enough to allow
anyone to exploit the Yanomami. As Bortoli says:

The question or problem for us is to make them very aware of the
dangers of certain change because they want to change everything,
and they see something they want, they want, they want. We want
to make them conscious of the dangers of certain changes. You
may have outboard motors but to keep the motor going you have
to have money to buy gasoline. And so we have to work more than
ever to make them aware of the consequences of change. We are
doing that. But even if you speak they to them, they have to touch
the experience. And they love when they have made an experience.
They come to you to speak to you about it again. You are seeing
what they are thinking now and so on. You want to be present in
this process.

To that extent that the instillation of this caution among the
Yanomami has made the Yanomami more difficult to work among,
Chagnon is correct in stating that the Salesians have made his
research more difficult. However, this caution is a necessary
ingredient in the world in which they live, for the threat of illegal
miners and the slaughter in 1993 are very real issues. The lust for
Yanomami land among many Brazilians and Venezuelans is very

concrete as is the danger of epidemic disease carried into their area by outsiders. The outside world even begrudges the Yanomami the resources and their cost required to fight these endemic diseases.

Teo Marcano, a physician who served for five years in the High Orinoco, summed up the situation in the following manner:

> Now we are preparing a system to supplement the health of the Yanomami. There is no continuing health service there. It is very expensive. You have to spend more money on the few thousand Yanomami then among the many people in Puerto Ayucucho. The Ministry of Health has to spend more money among the Yanomami than among other peoples. The Yanomami don't vote. They don't produce anything. When you try to make a proposal to the major foundations, they ask you "For who are the Yanomami relevant?" (Marcano 1994).

Reflections

While peace between anthropologists and missionaries is undoubtedly a very desirable thing, to an anthropological outsider it is clear that the message the missionaries send is often not the one their audience always receives. Missionaries are well aware that cultural differences in both the encoding and decoding of a message as well as in the "medium" through which the message travels hinder and distort its reception and interpretation. Too often, however, they tend to think of "culture" occurring at some "macro level," almost as a massive penumbra enshrouding a body of people. It is far more meaningful to visualize "culture" as being created in individual interpersonal encounters as well as in the expectations each participant brings to such encounters.

Luzbetak (1988:124), among the most anthropologically oriented of all missiologists, states clearly:

> If Christ were not unique and universal, normative and final, most of what the present author understands as mission, whether in non-Christian or Christian lands, would make little sense indeed. A unique and universal Christ is what the Gospel is all about, current radical theologians notwithstanding. ON this\single basic theological

premise alone much that an anthropologist may or may not have
to suggest will depend.

The *ad hoc* contextualization often made in mission fields
because of pastoral concerns frequently adds to the mixed message
of the mission. After all, if one "respects" the old ways then why are
some acceptable and others not? Why agree that God is found in
all religions but refuse to let one be Christian, Muslim, and traditionalist at the same time? Why are the modernization tendencies
of Christianity so inherently opposed to traditional relations?

Finally, unanswerably, many indigenous people ask, "Why do you
wish to give us a version of Christianity so different from that
practiced in your own country?" Even the remotest parts of the
world are now well within the world communication network.
Without doubt many people became Christians in order to gain
perceived advantages elsewhere in the world. Not all perceived
advantages, however, are material. Many are psychological. Others
are, in fact, defensive. Too many of these needs, desires, and expectations are simply out-of-awareness. Culturally, they are merely
taken for granted. The fact that a missionary does not always understand these demands in the cultural terms of the people is not a
problem of good-will. It is a problem of cultural translation. Good
will alone cannot avoid mixed messages resulting from conflicting
structural and cultural categories.

The missionary-anthropologist Kenelm Burridge warns, furthermore, that

> Official statements of ideals and tolerance collide with new ways of
> thinking, fresh attitudes to the world, and differing dispositions that
> require new institutions and structures to contain them. Respect for
> institutions and respect for persons are not necessarily tied together
> (Burridge 1991: 200).

A major theme of Burridge's perceptive study is the persistent
uncertainty found in even the most positive statements of cultural
respect on the part of Christian organizations. Reservations
regarding practices opposed to missionary perceived essence of
Christianity, usually those involving polygyny, are maintained. I
repeat that "the past" is used to promote various agendas and that

no imputation of ill-will is necessary to understand the dynamics of the social situation and competition.

Cox (1991), moreover, reminds us that cultures are changing at a dazzling pace and that those missionaries who advocate a return to "traditional" beliefs may, in some sense, provoke modernizing peoples to accuse them of cultural imperialism, as Mbefo (1987), has, in fact, done. Moreover, it is also imperative to note that no culture is a unified object and that people have always used aspects of their cultural heritage to promote their desired goals.

The question at issue is "In what sense can we say that a culture is `authentic`? Who, for example, defines the terms of authenticity (McDonald 1993)? We are long past regarding any culture as consistent and unified. The concept of hegemony has alerted us to consider the terms of discourse and to be alert to who sets those terms.

Unquestionably, we automatically inquire "Authentic for whom?" Similarly, we regard culture as in one sense or other as a communication system. Therefore, we not only seek to discover for whom it is authentic but under what conditions and for what purpose it may be so. The audience equally contributes to its interpretation and social actors, willingly or not, present a particular version of their "culture," or more accurately from their cultural repertoire, to fit their particular audience. From a transactional, symbolic-interactionist, perspective, they do so in hopes of attaining some perceived good and, perhaps, to avoid some discerned evil.

This line of inquiry consequently seeks to discover how a "genuine" or "authentic" culture helps people solve problems. It appears necessary to distinguish in what manner a people distinguishes what constitute problems and how they apply "cultural" solutions to those problems. In that sense, therefore, the concept of "authentic" culture emerges as an adaptive one in so far as it directs our attention to the manner in which people use aspects of their cultural repertoire to adapt to particular self-defined problems. Since culture, so conceived, enables people to adapt to specific settings it is an evolutionary concept in keeping with its ever-changing kaleidoscopic nature.

Any attempt to address these dilemmas takes us into deep-seated regions of the psychology and culture of missionaries. Missionaries deserve the same type of intensive ethnographic work we extend to any other group. Such work would profitably begin through distinguishing the differences found among missionaries in terms of national origin, religion, age, sex, location of work, personality, education, and other relevant variables. This information would move us toward greater understanding of cultural processes.

In fact, the missionary, in league with many anthropologists, is at heart a romantic who does not wish to see "his people" become "too" modern. At the same time, he knows he "cannot retard progress." The message he sends others is often mixed because his own internal message is itself confused. I use "he" consciously, for women missionaries are much clearer in their mission.[19] There are hints that African and Euroamerican clergy have begun to move in that direction. So far their efforts have not produced a "paganization" of Christianity. Rather, these efforts have led to a deeper appreciation of its universality. Incarnation theology and a deeper understanding of liturgical reform have led the way toward a true merger of traditions.

Culture is, among other things, a pattern for living and a means for adapting to an ever-changing cultural environment, a position explicitly stated in *Gaudium et Spes* (1965) which asserted that the Church "is not tied exclusively or indissolubly to any race or nation, to any one particular way of life, or to any customary practices, ancient or modern". Therefore, questions regarding its authenticity degenerate into mere Platonic quibbles for those with political axes to grind while the *real* people who live their own authentic lives somehow realize that whatever gets them through their days is authenticity enough.

Conclusion

At root the Salesian-Chagnon dispute was a fraternal struggle, a struggle between two branches of the family. One branch seeking truth in what is apparent only through empirical methods; the other, through a metaphysical method. Each, perhaps secretly, envies the other his means to certainty while each must deal with his own internal demons and doubts. The conflict was not truly about rifles, depletion of hunting resources, nor the best means, if any, to promote sustainable development. It was about the human condition itself and fear of seeing one's self in the other.

Missionaries and anthropologists in spite of their protests share a number of characteristics. Both, for example, claim spiritual descent from figures in classical antiquity; missionaries from St. Paul and anthropologists from Herodotus. Both witnessed a rebirth of their professions during the Renaissance as new peoples impressed themselves upon European consciousness in a manner previously unknown. Indeed, many "new" trends in both missiology and anthropology had their roots during the classic and Renaissance periods, including the current missionary concept of "inculturation" theology and the anthropologist's preoccupation with reflexivity. Finally, both established images dominant in the popular mind during the late nineteenth and early twentieth centuries; namely, that of idealistic adventurers who travel to remote and exotic places to serve an aspiration outside of oneself. Once established, that image has been virtually impervious to any changes that have occurred since.[20]

I have written previously of the contradictory relationship that exists between missionaries and anthropologists and of the great debt anthropologists owe to missionaries for much of their work (Salamone 1994, 1983, 1982, 1977). I suggest that one of the reasons for the uncertainty of missionary-anthropologist relationships stems from their theoretical disagreements. Moreover, I further suggest that many of the theoretical disagreements between anthropologists and missionaries are more apparent than real, stemming from motives not deeply related to theoretical issues at all but having more to do with boundary-maintaining mechanisms and self-definition or more material motives. In either case, their disagreements have more to do with power struggles for perceived scarce resources than with abstruse conceptual formulations. Missionaries, typically, spend far more time in the field than do anthropologists. Their language skills generally surpass those of anthropologists and their relationships with indigenous peoples tend to be of longer and deeper dimensions than do those of anthropologist. On the other hand, their purpose in being in the field, in spite of some demurrers, is to change the people with whom they come into contact. Specifically, it is to change their world view, converting both the people and their world-view to their own religion and understanding of the world. Their understanding of the people's cosmology and way of life, therefore, at least in theory, is mainly for the purpose of changing them to their own version of western cosmology and behavior. Generally, anthropologists have looked rather cynically at missionaries and their objectives.

In common with other nineteenth and twentieth century rationalists, Sir James Frazer was a curious mixture of Rationalist/ Romantic. Certainly, he shared the contemporary fascination with "exotic" practices. These practices were carefully displayed in their full glory for all to wonder over. Practices from hither and yon found themselves cheek-by-jowl with one another to suit Frazer's grand evolutionary scheme.

Conversely, however, Frazer placed contemporary practices alongside exotica from areas foreign to the European world. His point appears to be to demonstrate that underneath the apparent surface differences there was an underlying communal reality uniting these "strange" practices. That shared reality Frazer attributed to "the psychic unity of mankind," meaning not only that all humans share a common humanity but that given similar circumstances they will arrive at similar solutions to life's problems. Although it is a rather mechanistic view of human behavior and mental processes, it does have the virtue of including the "savage races" within the human family. At times, in fact, Frazer even seems to glance nostalgically at a certain lost innocence no longer within the grasp of "scientific man" of his day.

It is this powerful evocation of "the savage," as well as his generally reverberant literary style, that has enabled Frazer to withstand powerful attacks from within and outside anthropology while influencing professional and amateur anthropologists. My point is that Frazer has inspired missionaries and anthropologists in numerous ways and that a study of their movement away from his direct sway holds one key for understanding the trajectory of missionary-anthropologist relationships. Here I wish to focus on Frazer's treatment of magic and religion and the manner in which exploration of that false dichotomy has developed in anthropological and missiological thought.

For Frazer (1963:11-12), it is clear, magic and religion were contrasting categories, sharing only the fact that they were erroneous ways of thinking about reality. Magic, moreover, differentiated itself from religion as "savages" began to notice the first glimmerings of natural law. To paraphrase Malinowski, who acknowledged his debt to Frazer even while differing with him on numerous issues, "Magic compels, religion requests." Magic was simply false science, based on faulty empirical observation. It would, under the right circumstances, evolve into true science but its basic orientation was scientific not religious. It is true that magic frequently attempted to influence spiritual beings or powers whose existence could not be empirically verified, but both Malinowski and Frazer attributed that as part of the cultural milieu of various people and focused on the procedures used in addressing these beings or powers (Malinowski 1948).

Malinowski's assertion that religion finds its own fulfillment in itself while magic is always for something other than itself, for good crops or a successful voyage, appealed greatly to missionaries who reversed Malinowski's progression and with Wilhelm Schmidt saw the movement from magic to religion as a devolutionary one, as evidenced by Schmidt's favorite example, the Pygmies (Schmidt 1935). They could ignore the fact that science, not religion, was the asserted logical mental perfection of magic and that religion for both Frazer and Malinowski was a dead-end side road. Some hope, moreover, could be taken from Frazer's conclusion to the *Golden Bough* (1963:826).

The reality in the "grounded world," however, is somewhat different from that of the more logical "typical" or "ideal" one. It is that "grounded world," the phenomenological reality and the use partisan actors make of theoretical constructs which I have explored in this paper. At that level basic behavioral similarities stand out in stark relief from those divergent philosophical positions which biased actors employ to underpin and "explain" them. In sum, I contend that anthropologists and missionaries are truly squabbling siblings who share a Romantic ancestry, as distasteful as the thought may be to many members of either camp.

> Brighter stars will rise on some voyager of the future - some great Ulysses of the realms of thought - than shine on us. The dreams of magic may one day be the waking realities of science. But a dark shadow lies athwart the far end of this fair prospect. For however vast the increase of knowledge and of power which the future may have in store for man, he can scarcely hope to stay the sweep of those great forces which seem to be making silently but relentlessly

for the destruction of all this starry universe in which our earth swims as a speck or mote. In the ages to come man may be able to predict, perhaps even to control, the wayward courses of the winds and clouds, but hardly will his puny hands have strength to speed afresh our slackening planet in its orbit or rekindle the dying fire of the sun. Yet the philosopher who trembles at the idea of such distant catastrophes may console himself by reflecting that those gloomy apprehensions, like the earth and the sun themselves, are only parts of that unsubstantial world which thought has conjured up out of the void, and that the phantoms which the subtle enchantress has evoked to-day she may ban tom-morrow. They too, like so much that to common eyes seems solid, may melt into air, into thin air.

To the religious mind that beautiful and poetic conclusion evinced a despair with mere rationality and its inevitably logical tragic resolution. The poet T. S. Eliot, after all, was of a rather conservative religious inclination but as Bartholomeusz (1991;340-41) indicates Eliot took what he needed from Frazer, especially the myth of the dying god, and transformed it for his own needs. In Eliot's hands the religious elements in *The Waste Land* stand in stark contrast with science's destruction of the mystery and majesty of the world. I suggest that missionaries used Frazer in a similar manner. [21]

After all, if one "respects" the old ways then why are some acceptable and others not? Why agree that God is found in all religions but refuse to let one be Christian, Muslim, and traditionalist at the same time? Why are the modernization tendencies of Christianity so inherently opposed to traditional relations? Finally, unanswerably, they ask,"Why do you wish to give us a version of Christianity so different from that practiced in your own country?"

As anthropologists point out, inherently the mission situation is structured so that its consequences flow inevitably from the virtually unavoidable actions of its protagonists. The mission protagonists do appear to outsiders as somewhat larger than life. "The Missionary" and the "Indigene" represent types, categories of our Western epistemology. Their "fatal flaws," virtues in other settings, lead to misunderstanding that cause epic suffering. Character truly becomes destiny as West meets Third World and each fails to understand the other in spite of the best of intentions.

The Chagnon-Salesian controversy is part of this overall process within the nature of anthropology itself. It is part of the history of the field that sees it as moving toward a new future for those "savages" entrusted to its care. The missionary, on the other hand views the indigene as an opportunity to spread the word of God and perfect the message the "savage" has received in some primordial manner. That neither the anthropologist nor missionary wishes the "native" harm is part of the tragedy of life itself. That the Yanomami, in common with other Fourth World peoples, needs to be protected from the dangers of development by those who, however well-intentioned, have their own agendas is also part of their own personal tragedy.

It is from the perspective of tragedy that one should view the Chagnon-Salesian controversy, a tragedy rooted in so ancient a transgression that like that which shadowed the House of Atreus it is doomed to continue into the distant future with periods of truce among its combatants. Like Yanomami warfare itself, it is marked by truces, shifting alliances, and betrayals. Like Yanomami warfare also it is often the innocent who suffer, the weak who are most harmed. Finally, like Yanomami warfare it is conducted to gain and control strategic resources, not always material but always precious.

Chapter 3

The Yanomami: Fierce People
or Fierce Interpreters?

Frank A. Salamone

The Yanomami are among the more famous groups in ethno-graphic history. Indeed, battles over the correct interpretation of Yanomami life are almost as famous as the people themselves. Due mainly to the writing of Napoleon Chagnon (1968) and more recently to the book and National Geographic special by Kenneth Good (1992), the Yanomami became classroom favorites, known to thousands of college freshmen and those who watch television specials on "exotic peoples." As Chagnon, perhaps somewhat immodestly but with a great deal of truth, says:

> My work on the Yanomami made them instantly famous, perhaps the most famous tribe in the world. That made them very attractive to a lot of anthropologists (Winkler 1994: A18).

More importantly for the Yanomami, however, is the fact that their "fame" has been a valuable weapon in their self-preservation against the inroads of threats from modernization; such as the influx of illegal gold miners and development schemes that would destroy the ecological basis of their lives.

There are approximately 22,500 Yanomami in the Amazon Basin, making them the largest indigenous group there. These Indians are spread among roughly 225 villages in Venezuela and Brazil in an area in the Amazon rain forest to the north of the Amazon River (Winkler 1994: A18). Each Yanomami village is autonomous but has alliances with other villages. These villages carry on warfare with other villages periodically. There have been bitter disputes regarding just how frequently these clashes occur.

Within the last few years a large number of Yanomami have died from malaria, respiratory diseases, measles, and other endemic diseases. Many of these diseases have been introduced by outside populations. Still other Yanomami have been killed in clashes with miners and other agents of "civilization." These clashes with outsiders have led to noisy arguments within anthropology in particular and in development circles in general regarding the best ways in which to safeguard them. At times, it appeared that the interests or desires of the Yanomami themselves were being over-looked as one faction or another attacked the position of their opponents. Each faction purported to speak for the Yanomami. In the following sections, I intend to give the student an introduction to enough ethnographic material about the Yanomami to enable them to evaluate the arguments that follow in the remainder of the book.

The Yanomami Way of Life

Given the many controversies regarding the interpretation of the Yanomami way of life and even the basic details of that life, it is important to attempt to present as clear a picture as possible of their general way of life and what is known of their pre-contact history. Currently, more than 95% of the Yanomami live in their traditional environment, deep in the Amazon forest. The rest live along rivers. These latter expand less effort than their fellow Yanomami on inland hunting. Fishing - more dependent on trade goods such as lights, hooks and lines, and canoes - has replaced inland hunting. These riverine Yanomami can settle more perma-nently on their farm lands. Their use of canoes also allows them to expand available farming areas, since they can cross the river to plant new gardens.

More commonly, however, Yanomami live within the forest, dividing their time between horticulture and hunting and gathering. Horticulture is garden farming using hoes or digging sticks. It requires intensive labor rather than extensive fields. Even so, Kenneth Good (1995) states that Yanomami men spend no more than an average of two hours per day on their fields. Since they could more easily spend more time on their fields, thereby increasing their plantain or sweet potato production by doubling their farming time without disturbing other aspects of their lives, the question obviously arises as to why they do not.

The answer to that question provides a key to understanding the Yanomami way of life. How an anthropologist answers it determines how she or he will come to understand the Yanomami in particular and cultural life in general.

Let us begin with some indisputable facts. The Yanomami live in villages that range in size from 40 to 300 people. No matter the size, the villages are very public places. As Chagnon (1983:4) states:

> One can hear, see, and smell almost everything that goes on anywhere in the village. Privacy is rare, but sexual discreetness is possible in the garden or at night while others sleep.

These villages are separated from their neighbors by many miles of uninhabited area. This spacing allows the game to increase, expanding the available meat for the community. It also serves to minimize conflict with other groups while allowing disgruntled members of a village to establish a new village.

Because the majority of Yanomami, about 95% of them, are not sedentary, they spend a good deal of their time trekking. Most of their treks take place in the dry season since the wet season floods the jungle and makes voyaging burdensome. Good estimates that they trek, go on a *wayumi*, on an average of 40% of their time. In some cases, they spend up to 60% of their time trekking. There is no doubt that this trekking serves some useful functions for the Yanomami. Trekking, for example, keeps families together. Treks, moreover, produce about twice as much food as simply hunting near gardens. Consumption of wild food reaches about 70% on treks.

There are other significant advantages to trekking. Treks help provide a cooling off period after quarrels, many of which result from disputes over appropriate meat sharing. Since meat is the only item shared village-wide, failure to receive a perceived equal share can cause great friction in a village. On a trek the village can split. Each section can use the trek as a cooling off period. Moreover, smaller groups have the advantage of making for better foraging. Additionally, these smaller groups tend to plant new gardens, expanding the cultivated area, increasing the chances for peaceful splits and wider ties in the area among Yanomami. Finally, trekking can be used as an evasive technique to avoid raids from an enemy village.

Trekking also produces problems. When returning from a trek it is not uncommon for a village to discover that other villages have eaten their food. Unless compensation is offered, the offended village will seek revenge. That revenge can take the form of chest pounding, club fights, or raids. Practices which Napoleon Chagnon has clearly described in his *Yanomamo: The Fierce People*.

Chest pounding duels involve members of the quarreling villages challenging one another to individual combat. Each man takes his turn pounding on his opponent's chest with his bare fist. No emotion is to be shown nor any sign of pain in the duel. It is the mildest of the various conflict resolution battles. Club fighting, however, is the next level of combat and involves participants from the quarreling factions to fighting on separate sides with clubs. The stakes have obviously gone up.

Failure to solve the problem by these means can lead to warfare. Generally, groups of allied villages may raid their enemies. These raids are just that; namely, hit and run forays against an enemy. There is no pitched battle with clearly drawn sides. There is an ambush against members of the other side in which any member is fair game. There are variations on this theme, which Chagnon has deftly described. For example, a group may be invited to a feast and then killed at that feast because of festering differences between the villages.

Notice, however, that a simple listing of functions and dysfunctions of trekking avoids the central issue; namely, *why do the Yanomami trek?* Good (1995 and 1987) lines up with Marvin Harris (1984) on this issue and against Chagnon's (1988 and 1968) position.

Specifically, Good and Harris suggest that even though the Yanomami are horticulturalists, they cannot supply their required protein needs. Their basic food crops, plantains and bananas, introduced by the conquistadors, do not supply sufficient protein to meet their nutritional needs. However, because of their partial sedentarization their population has increased from about 25 people to 60-70 people per village. Because of this population growth, they can no longer survive as simply hunters and gatherers. Neither can they subsist as full time farmers. Therefore, they trek. While they trek, fields can continue producing food.

Therefore, according to Good and Harris, they trek because of a need to solve the problems caused by protein deficiency. They do not have sufficient protein in their diets. Because game species in the Amazon are relatively small, they are quickly depleted. Men can go on long distance hunts for a week. But treks produce about twice as much protein and keep families together.

In this light, feasts take on a new perspective. They are means for sharing a rare resource, meat, and for establishing paths for safe expansion into new horticultural and hunting areas. Warfare, which Chagnon (1988 and 1968) so ably describes, is the breakdown of negotiations necessitated by a search for adequate protein. It is also, sometimes, the result of grievances that accumulate as a result of the quest for protein.

Ferguson (1995 and 1993) relates Chagnon's portrayal of the Yanomami to the "killer ape" theories that were so much in the air at the time. These theories sought a biological explanation for human aggression, a gene for warfare as a means for survival and human adaptation. The apparent isolation of the Yanomami lends fuel to that theory. After all, if the Yanomami had no contact until about 1950 with Europeans or Euro-Americans, Chagnon was viewing a pristine group of people, unaffected by outside forces. That which he observed, therefore, was in some way "the original state of humans." If they fought because of some innate aggression, then warfare and conflict were the biological lot of the human species and attempts to alter that innate drive were doomed to failure. Chagnon's development of these ideas in his sociobiological mate selection theory in which the more effective killer gets to mate more frequently than less aggressive people was but a variation on that theme.

Ferguson is a bit gentler to those who propose an alternate theory of cultural adaptation for Yanomami warfare. These people, among them Good and Harris, explain Yanomami warfare as a means for keeping down the population in the face of scarce protein supply. Warfare "spaced groups" far enough apart across the rain forest to lessen their competition. Warfare "contributed to the Yanomami's ability to survive within the limitation of their ecosystem."

However, Ferguson states that Yanomami have been influenced by Europeans for 350 years and that their warfare can only be understood in that light. In the 1630s Spanish, Dutch, Portuguese slave raiding and that of their indigenous allies strongly affected the Yanomami. Slave-raiding wiped out the more densely settled chiefdoms in the Yanomami area while restricting them to highland sanctuaries. In Ferguson's view, the Yanomami were not hunters and gatherers immediately before the coming of the Europeans. What we view today among 95% of the Yanomami is an adaptation to marginality forced on them through European contact.

Moreover, he argues, from the mid-18th century until 1950 peaceable and violent contacts with outsiders have been virtually continuous. In 1950 the first Protestant mission, a New Tribes station, was established in Yanomami territory. That station is still in existence. Shortly after the Salesians founded their own station in the High Orinoco area. That station has also has had a continuous existence. Needless to say, these stations have had a great influence but they are part of a long-term Western contact with the Yanomami.

Ferguson sees a relationship between Yanomami wars and changes in relationships with Euro-American contact. These wars, in his view, are related to control of or access to trade goods.

> Like other Amazonian groups, the Yanomami have rapidly come to regard steel tools, aluminum pots, cloth, and other manufactured items as necessities. Yanomami able to obtain these goods close to the source want them not only for their own use but also to trade with groups farther away. In exchange, other Yanomami provide local products, labor, wives, and political support (Ferguson 1995:62)

These trade relationships, according to Ferguson, cause friction because of their inequality and essential nature. These frictions lead to raiding and warfare. Ferguson argues that through warfare Yanomami seek to consolidate, protect, or improve a group's position in the trade network. Although many examples could be put forth to establish the point, that of the growth of rubber trading, however, provides a fine example.

In the early 1900s there was a rapid increase in rubber tapping along the Uraricoera and other rivers near the Brazilian Yanomami. This activity led to an increase in the supply of Western trade goods. Predictably, the incidence of "violence" increased as local Yanomami established a trade position in the increased flow of goods. Once they settled down, they, in turn, were pressed by "'wild' Yanomami in the mountains."

Social Organization and Structure

Anthropologists generally use the term "social organization" to refer to the actual activities and behavior that make up daily life while they use "social structure" most frequently to direct attention to the more idealized relationship or model of the correlations of the various parts of society. "Social organization" is a more concrete concept while " social structure" is an abstraction from it. Another way to conceptualize the concepts is to note that "social organization" refers to process while "social structure" refers to form. Both are essential to understanding society and culture just as anatomy and physiology are to understanding biology.

Chagnon (1983) uses village fissioning to organize his discussion of social organization while Alcida Rita Ramos (1995) uses time and space. Each approach has its advantages and approaches similar material from different perspectives. Specifically, both Chagnon and Ramos look at daily social life, gender relations, adult-child relationships, economic activities, and other aspects of daily life. Both go on to view aspects of social rules, the area of social structure; namely, marriage, kinship, residence rules, social control and leadership. Both are concerned with culture change. Interestingly, Ramos does not discuss warfare and her discussion of internal conflict is much more muted than that of Chagnon. In general, however, their description of daily life is relatively similar and conforms in basic detail to that of Albert (1985, 1992), Hulme (1988), Lizot (1973, 1975, 1976, 1984, 1985), Smole (1976), Taylor (1974, 1976, 1977, 1981), among others.

There is a status ranking among the Yanomami. Males outrank females. Thus, unsurprisingly, the Yanomami trace descent through the father's line and males and females who have the same father belong to his clan. A clan is a descent group traced through one parent's line, in this case father's father and so on back to an unknown or mythical founder. This clan membership eases relationships and governs marriage choices. (Ramos 1995: 57-66).

In general, women have little to say about to whom they are married and many marriages are arranged before a girl reaches puberty. Women do work that men consider beneath them; such as, carrying firewood and hauling water. According to Chagnon, women should anticipate the wishes of their spouses. Men can beat their wives but there are limits on their mistreatment.

A woman's brothers protect her from mistreatment. Chagnon states that women fear being taken in raids because they may be taken far from their brothers' protection. Therefore, women exercise one of their weapons, ridicule, to protect themselves from being victims of raids. They do so through taunting their men to be fierce and avenge wrongs so that others may view them as "fierce" and not to be taken lightly.

All writers agree that marriages play vital political roles in cementing relationships and forging alliances. In that regard, the Yanomami differ little from other similar groups, including many in our own society. Marriages set up and strengthen relationships between family groups. Not surprisingly, the preferred marriage is what anthropologists term "bilateral cross-cousin" marriage; that is, children of siblings of the opposite sex on both mother's or father's side. In simple English, it means that I, as a man, would marry a cousin who was my mother's brothers daughter or my father's sister's daughter; that is, my cross-cousin. A woman would marry a cousin who was her mother's brother's son or father's sister's son. Sister-exchange, from a male point of view, tends to tie the village together and prevent conflict while forming alliances. In actual practice, a high number of marriages conform to this practice.

Ramos states that about 70% of her Sanuma villages in Brazil meet this description.

In common with many other societies, the Yanomami are polygynous. Polygyny is a form of polygamy, plural marriage, in which a man has two or more wives at the same time. In addition to being a form of status marker (the more wives a man has the higher his prestige) polygyny also provides for women and children. If Chagnon's estimates of male deaths among the Yanomami in warfare is accurate, roughly 40% of the men, then polygyny as a form of protection for women and children takes on added meaning.

Children are very precious to the Yanomami and require a great deal of protection since they are more vulnerable than adults to supernatural dangers. Given the high incidence of disease in the area, which no one disputes, and the presence of raiding and outside invasion, it is easy to understand the Yanomami attitude toward children and the need to protect them physically and spiritually. Although there are differences of opinion regarding the meaning of Yanomami patience with children, no authority questions it. Therefore, one can only imagine Yanomami horror at the various massacres the modern age has inflicted on these children. Ramos (1995: 280) states the matter clearly.

> . . . sixteen Hashimu villagers of the upper Orinoco valley in Venezuela were murdered by a group of heavily armed Brazilian *garampeiros* (illegal gold miners). The brutality of the killings shocked the world. The victims, mostly children, were beheaded and pierced through with knives. The case was defined as genocide, and both Brazil and Venezuela joined efforts to punish the criminals. This event put the Yanomami back onto the media's front pages . . .

This slaughter was but the latest in a series of such genocidal attacks, most of whose victims are children.

The stage of childhood ends early for the Yanomami as with most traditional peoples. Chagnon states that by 10 years of age a girl is such an economic asset that she leaves childhood and spends a great deal of time working. A boy can extend his childhood to his late teens. In contrast, many young girls have children of their own by their late teens.

Similarly, it is obvious when a girl becomes physiologically mature. People mark her first menses with various rituals. She is isolated in her house and hidden behind a barrier of leaves. She changes clothing; her old cotton garments are destroyed and replaced by new ones made by her mother or older female friends. A young girl's food is fed to her by her relatives on a stick. She is forbidden to come into contact with food in any other manner. There are additional restrictions, relating to her manner of speech; in whispers, to whom she may speak, relatives; and her method of scratching, with a stick not used for her feeding.

Boys have no ritualized rite of passage marking their movement from childhood to adulthood. Chagnon uses anger at the use of one's personal name as a sign of movement to an adult stage.

> When the adults in the village cease using his personal name, they young man has achieved some sort of masculine adult status. Young men are always very touchy about their names and they, more than anyone else, take quick offense when hearing their names mentioned. The Yanomami constantly employ *teknonymy* when a kinship usage is ambiguous (Chagnon 1983: 115-116).

Teknonymy is the use of a kinship relationship is used to address a person. For example, in place of my personal name, Frank, I might be addressed as Angelo's son or Frances's son. Use of personal names among the Yanomami, especially among the Yanomami of Venezuela is not acceptable. However, a young man will object to being addressed as his father's son when he is striving to establish his position as a mature adult. Men, particularly, are careful to defend their honor through objecting to public use of their personal names. When people die, moreover, there is a taboo on the use of their names, forcing people to ingenious inventions for naming their children, as Chagnon notes. In fact, the most amusing section of his ethnography on the Yanomami concerns his problems with names in his construction of genealogies (Chagnon 1983: 18-20).

There are many other aspects of social organization and structure that take us into fascinating areas. These are well-covered in a number of works. I have tried here to whet the student's appetite and provide sufficient information to enable her or him to follow the basic arguments that follow. I cannot end, however, without some discussion of religion and culture change, for these are integral to understanding the gist of the debates that concern this text. Interested readers might want to refer to the following to pursue various other aspects of Yanomami life (Ferguson 1995, Ritchie 1996, Cocco 1972).

Religion

In common with other tribal peoples, there is not distinction between everyday life and religion such as Westerners commonly make. One realm fades into the other. One way to ease into the understanding is to consider the process of naming a child, or "hunting the name." This name becomes a "spirit name" and is sacred to the person throughout the length of his or her life. So important is finding an appropriate name that a man will risk violating the taboos of the *couvade*, sharing in the birth of the lying in at childbirth, to hunt an appropriate animal to capture its spirit.

The animal's spirit enters the child through its coccyx and the Yanomami expression, *humabi thabalima*, is best translated "the making of the coccyx (Ramos 1995: 216)." Before a child is born the *humabi* is in the animal in the forest. However, after it is born, the child's father goes into the forest to hunt the animal, bring it home tied up in a bundle of leaves. The parents cannot touch the animal nor eat it because it possesses their child's spirit. Moreover, not every child possesses this spirit.

In attempting to solve this and other puzzles, Ramos has come to this conclusion regarding Yanomami culture and religion.

> In the humabi hunt we find a theme that runs through other contexts where the Sanuma <a branch of the Yanomami> seem to create prohibitions in order to break them. Mother-in-law avoidance is broken when mother-in-law and son-in-law duel each other at the breakup of a marriage. . .name secrecy is suspended

> when a person is chosen as the referent in teknonymy. . . and
> hunting prohibition is halted when a father has to attend to the
> obligation of naming his child (Ramos 1995: 218).

This dangerous quality of the supernatural is not peculiar to the
Yanomami but rather more clearly portrayed in their culture than
in many others.

The role of shaman, for example, illustrates this danger rather
clearly. Anthropologists have borrowed the word "shaman" from the
Chuckchee of Siberia. It refers to a part time religious specialist
who serves as a healer for the people. In conformity with other
Yanomami practices, only men can become shamans or *shabari*. Any
man who so desires can train to become a shaman. A man's teacher
is an older man who instructs him in the appropriate rituals and
songs while aiding him to fast. The shaman in training must also
abstain from sex because the spirits (*hekura*) do not like sex. Since
one of an initiates aims is to attract hekura to reside in his chest, it
is clear that he must abstain from sex if he is to have any success in
this difficult undertaking.

There is a multitude of spirits and a good shaman has many
residing inside himself. He can also command them to do his will,
including the killing of others, especially children. Shamans use a
hallucinogen named *ebene*, a sort of snuff, to aid them in contacting
the spirits. The more adept a shaman, the less the snuff he needs to
snort. The *ebene* aids the shaman in singing the type of beautiful
songs the spirits love, for they do cherish beauty. To increase his
attraction to the spirits the shaman also decorates himself with
pigment, his best feathers, and other gorgeous decorations. While
the shaman gets high, the spirits join him in the process.

This ecstatic state is also a dangerous one, for some shamans
seize the opportunity the trance presents to settle old scores. As
Chagnon writes:

> The Yanomami attitude seems to be that one is not quite respon-
> sible for his acts if he is in communion with the *hekuru* and high on
> *ebene*. Thus, one occasionally sees timed men use the opportunity
> to become boisterous and at times violent - running around the
> village in a stupor, wild eyed and armed, threatening to shoot
> someone with an arrow or hack someone with a machete. . . one

of the men decapitated another with a single blow of his machete, provoking a violent fission in the village and a long war between the two related groups (Chagnon 1983: 109).

The fact that these men had a long history of enmity is rather significant in understanding the phenomenon.

In general, the Yanomami believe that the spirit world is rather like this one or vice-versa. There is a consistency in morality between the two worlds that is logically extended to behavior. This makes sense when one realizes that the Yanomami cosmos has four layers: an empty layer on top (*duku ka misi*), the sky layer (*hedu ka misi*), earth (*hhhei ka misi*), and the area below (*beita bebi*). Yanomami, specifically the people of Amahiri-teri, live there. The Amahiri-teri are rather unfortunate people. Their village fell to this level. Unfortunately, their forest did not. Consequently, the Amahiri-teri do not have sufficient food supplies and have turned to cannibalism. They seek the souls of children from the earth level. When they capture these souls, they take them to the lower level and devour them.

The Yanomami, as is typical, see things as a combination of opposites. Therefore, they abhor cannibalism but fear that humans will fall to that level. Chagnon notes how the jaguar disgusts them, and how Yanomami noting him eat rare steaks from a tapir accused him of wanting to become a cannibal (Chagnon 1983: 92). This duality is further seen in their account of the origin of the Amahiri-teri and the *hekura*.

> The Amahiri-teri people lived at the time of the *no badabo*, the original humans. These original humans were distinct from living Man in that they were part spirit and part human, and most were also part animal - and the myths frequently explain how this transformation occurred. When the original people died, they turned into spirits: *hekura*. The term *no badabo* means, literally, "those who are now dead." In the context of myth and stories of the cosmos, it means "the original humans" or "those who were here in the beginning of time (Chagnon 1983: 92).

I have given the student, once again, but a taste of the rich complexity of a Yanomami cultural domain. I have tried to confine myself to topics that will aid the student in understanding the debate that ensued concerning the interpretation of the Yanomami way of life. There is one other area that concerns the anthropologist and the missionary; namely, that which is termed endocannibalism. Endocannibalism is the eating of related people. It is distinguished from exocannibalism - the eating of those not related to you. The Yanomami practice endocannibalism.

Chagnon is correct in noting that neither form requires the consumption of an entire body. There are two general explanations to cannibalism current in anthropology. Marvin Harris (1977), for example, argues that at least some cannibalism - that of the Aztecs - can be understood as fulfilling a need to combat protein deficiency. Others, such as Chagnon, argue that it is a symbolic gesture in which one person seeks to meet ritualistic or religious goals; such as, communion with an ancestor or the attempt to acquire the courage of an enemy. This explanation seems to me to best decipher the Yanomami practice of "endocannibalistic anthropophagerphy;" that is, the consumption of their own dead. Yanomami honor their dead by drinking their cremated remains.

There are elaborate ritual prescriptions as to how the remains are to be drunk and who may or may not drink them. Further, precautions are taken against contamination of others as a result of the smoke produced during cremation. Children, especially, are vulnerable to contamination. Moreover, the ashes of those men killed in a raid are consumed only by women and their ashes may be preserved until a village feels it has avenged their death properly. These and other details are presented quite clearly by Chagnon (1983: 106).

Needless to say, there is a rather wide opinion among missionaries regarding Yanomami religious beliefs and practices. The Salesian fathers tend to be more accepting of their beliefs than more evangelical missionaries. They may even participate in drinking the ashes of the dead. They themselves often use tobacco and do not condemn shamanic use of hallucinogen (Chagnon 1983:210). Some of these difference, certainly, is a result of the culture of the missionaries as much of their different religions. The Salesians, for example, tend to be Spanish and Italian. The Evangelicals are mainly Americans from the midwestern and southern states.

The Yanomami, ultimately, will have to make the often painful adaptation that the centralized state requires of its people. Even a brief sketch of their religious practices demonstrates areas of potential conflict and reinterpretation. Once again, they illustrate a process that is being forced on marginalized peoples throughout the globe; namely, their painful incorporation into the centralized state and the world system. This is part of the process of culture change discussed in the concluding section of this introduction.

Politics and Government

In real life, the Yanomami do not separate one aspect of life from another. It is only in analysis that we separate religion, from kinship, from trade, or from any other aspect of cultural life. Thus, in discussing Yanomami political life and government, it is important to keep in mind the fact that all areas of Yanomami life enter into their government.

Each village is autonomous but has a series of trade and kinship relationships that link it to a broader network of alliances. No single person leads a Yanomami village, although there are people of influence who gain that influence through individual ability. Generally speaking, anthropologists term the Yanomami an egalitarian society rather than a rank, status, or hierarchical one. Basically, that means that there are as many prestigious positions as there are people to fill them. While women and young men may not be so sure about the egalitarian nature of the society, adult males do tend to see it as an achievement-based rather than an ascribed (inherited by birth) society. It is in this light that we can say that no one person does or can speak for the Yanomami.

If that statement is true for a village, where political decisions are taken as a result of consensus, it is even more true on broader regional or national levels. The Yanomami do not recognize a political body larger than the village. However, kinship and trade do link villages together. Ferguson (1995:30-35) discusses these links very carefully. Basically, the Yanomami attempt to monopolize the source of trade. Those villages that do so obtain great advantages in their trade relationships. Middlemen not only have a clear supply of both modern and traditional goods, they also build up their kinship ties with interior villages.

Since the principle of reciprocity, of exchange of favors, operates very strongly in Yanomami life, people with a trade advantage are also at an advantage in building up kinship obligations. As Ferguson (1995:33) phrases the matter: "The transformation of village exchange implies transformation of political alignments."

Control of trade released Yanomami men in those villages from performing tedious bride service and living in their bride's villages while performing a duty Yanomami males find burdensome. Thus, Lizot (1978:8-9) speaks of two types of Yanomami communities arising. Those that hold manufactured goods at the source and those who depend on political allies for access to those goods. The second group tend to become wife-givers while the first keep their women in the village. Since their tends to be a scarcity of women, the first group gains both power and prestige in the Yanomami political world.

Chagnon (1967:122) notes that "Trade reduces the possibility that one group will attack the other without serious, overt provocation." Trade, therefore, is an integral part of the political process. It helps ensure peace between otherwise independent villages and provides a stimulus to the Yanomami's main political forum, the intervillage feast. At this feast, many political issues are resolved, cemented by trade and marriage arrangements.

The question of Yanomami fierceness enters logically into the issue of Yanomami government. Basically, fierceness refers to the Yanomami concept of *waiteri* (Chagnon 1967:124-126). It refers to a Yanomami's willingness to fight or to apply force. Thus, if a village is willing to apply force, go to war, against another village it is "fierce." Ferguson ties this willingness to apply force to other necessary factors: supply of Western goods at the source, ties of a source village to powerful Westerners who may back their favorite chief, the possession of shotguns, and the number of combatants on either side. Note that the Yanomami cannot really control the basic factors in this equation; namely, Western support and ecological limits on population. The increasing presence of the West in their area cannot but change their political structure in the present and future as it has in the past.

Culture Change and Its Consequences

Approximately 5% of the total Yanomami population have begun to lead sedentary lives along the Orinoco River, many near mission settlements. The well-being of these Indians is a primary topic of discussion between Chagnon and the missionaries. It is a legitimate question whether their presence has led to increased or decreased physical well-being. It is also a question that concerns missionaries as much as anthropologists.

I think it is generally true that the sedentarized Yanomami are more "peaceful" than others. It is equally true that hunting has depleted the local game supply in settled areas, forcing more sedentary Yanomami to turn to fishing for their protein needs. They also must turn to mission food and an increased reliance on cultivation. In turn, this change in adaptation has led to certain losses, including loss of conflict resolution mechanisms. It is no longer easy to go trekking to solve internal friction. There is less meat to share within the group as a result of decreased hunting There is loss of a traditional means for avoiding conflict; namely, the custom of meat sharing and its enhancement of solidarity. Additionally, sedentary Yanomami are prone to new diseases, mainly those brought into the area by Europeans. Thus, there is an increase in measles, influenza and other respiratory diseases as well as dental problems.

Unsurprisingly, violence may reach a level where it appears to be "normal." Ferguson states that such was the situation with the Yanomami with whom Chagnon came into contact in the early 1960s. These were Yanomami who had been subjected to forces, such as epidemics and trade disruptions, that had destroyed much of their "traditional" way of life. Jockeying for trade positions in the movement of Western goods, seeking to protect themselves from the forces the centralized state unleashed while being victims of Western diseases against which they had no protection produced such upheaval that interpersonal violence provided a means for attempting to cope with an uncertain world.

Good (1995:65) focuses on another less problematic aspect of culture contact, that between Brazilian miners and the Yanomami along the Venezuelan-Brazilian border. The Brazilian policy of encouraging development in the Amazon has led to devastation among the Yanomami and other indigenous Amazonian peoples. Catlle ranchers, miners, loggers, and farmers have destroyed the area. The rivers are poisoned by the effects of gold mining while the destruction of the rain forest is common knowledge.

The effects of the centralized state have reached into remote areas beyond its certain control. Ferguson states the matter succinctly:

> The impact of disease, trade goods, migrations, and political restructurings can spread far in advance of face-face contact, and when the state's advance agents do arrive, they commonly bring even more destruction with them (Ferguson 1995: 63).

Sadly, missionaries and anthropologists who do belong to that modern state system, get enmeshed in this web. Both have trade goods in their possession as the New Tribes, Salesians, and Chagnon discovered. Some have firearms as well, as the Chagnon-Salesian dispute revealed. However, it must be noted that failure to meet Yanomami expectations also arouses their ire against an anthropologist or missionary.

Ferguson notes one major aspect of culture change in the tribal zone. What Westerners smugly term "tribal warfare" is frequently the result of forces unleashed by Westerners, forces tied to global developments. Foreign intrusion can create or sharpen conflicts where none or few existed in the past. Ironically, Westerners have often used the conflicts which their presence provokes to advance what they term "civilization."

Colby and Dennett (1995) argue this point rather well in their book *Thy Will Be Done: The Conquest of the Amazon: Nelson Rockefeller and Evangelism in the Age of Oil*. As one reviewer, Bill Weinberg (1996:29) states:

> Gerard Colby and Charlotte Dennett argue the case for the existence of a century long de facto cooperative arrangement between the Rockefeller empire and the most effective, ambitious and zealous of fundamentalist missionary groups. Their common challenge was the post-World War II pacification of the new frontiers of the developing world -especially the Amazon rain forest.

Academics, including, one must sadly report, anthropologists, are not spared either. Colby and Dennett document the involvement of Cornell University in the C.I.A.'s anthropological and linguistic sponsored research in Peru. To anthropology's credit, however, a number of its members went on record in 1971 at the hemispheric World Council of Churches meeting in Barbados warning of a new age of Indian genocide and protesting the involvement of the Wycliffe's Summer Institute of Linguistic's involvement in Rockefeller's exploitation of indigenous peoples. They were joined by Catholics influenced by the emerging Liberation Theology that focuses on empowerment of native peoples in controlling their own lives. The Summer Institute of Linguistics has rejected these charges but it is clear that indigenous peoples and their supporters no longer assume the automatic benefits of western development. The Yanomami case clearly points the way to understanding this important lesson of the double-edged nature of the advance of progress. Moreover, anthropologists and missionaries are being forced to become more culturally sensitive the perceptions and wishes of the people among whom they work. No longer can they assume that they can work in isolation and represent the interests of "exotic' groups like the Yanomami to the outside world.

In keeping with a major idea of this book that the Yanomami are the appropriate people to speak for themselves, this introduction concludes with an excerpt from an interview with Davi Kopenawa reproduced in Ramos (1995:297).

When the gold miners came, some Yanomami were, unwisely, happy to have them around. They were thinking, without knowing them: "Maybe the gold miners are good people." They liked their food. The gold miners began to lure them with rice, manioc flour, and old clothes. The Yanomami didn't think much of the old clothes, but the gold miners kept giving them some of their food and they were happy to eat it. They stopped working their plots of land and planting their own food. Soon, all of them grew very ill. Then they began to die, all the old people died, and the Yanomami were very frightened. These Yanomami had no goods trade; they were isolated, they didn't have machetes or knives, which is why they came to the gold miners' camps in the first place. If they had enough of these things, they wouldn't have come anywhere near the gold miners . . . When the white people came, they shot the

Indians and caused them to die of epidemics. So, I am not at peace. We are not at peace.

Student Questions

1. How can the same ethnographic "facts" be interpreted in so many different ways?

2. What aspects of the Yanomami way of life would ease their transition to integration in the modern state?

3. What aspects of the Yanomami way of life would hinder their transition to integration in the modern state?

4. What are the positive and negative aspects of culture change among the Yanomami?

5. What can be done to improve the Yanomami chances for survival in the modern age?

Chapter Four

Yanomami Health Problems

Teodoro Marcano

My background is in tropical medicine and infectious disease. I work in a community health program that the Venezuelan government started in 1986 to study the main causes of Yanomami mortality. The major cause of death is simple malaria. The Yanomami live in a major malarial region. Unlike West Africans, the Yanomami have no genetic protection against malaria; they have nothing comparable to the sickling trait.

Another cause of death among Yanomami children is diarrhea. Not only because they are poorly nourished, or because the children become dehydrated but also because the Yanomami believe that diarrhea comes from witchcraft. Therefore, they usually don't bother to go to a western doctor. They go to the local doctor. When the local doctor has failed they come to us. This delay causes a real problem because we obtain the patient in the last condition and there may be nothing we can do at that time.

Hepatitis B is another major cause of death. This is very real problem among the Yanomami. Hepatitis B is infects a large number of Yanomami. About 80% of, die from either hepatitis B or malaria. There is little we can do for this kind of virus.

The first thing that I tried to do when I came to the area was learn all about Yanomami medicine. I had to do so before I could teach anything. Learning about Yanomami medicine is very hard because the causes of disease in the Yanomami system is very different in the western system. For example, the Yanomami conception of pain is quite complex. There are many forms of pain, depending on location and intensity.

I try to work together with the local doctor. I call the local doctor into the clinic but Yanomami don't believe in our medicine. They believe in their own medicine. Therefore, I attempt to retain the patient as long as possible. Otherwise they will not continue to keep any bandages sterile or even change them once the leave the clinic. Nevertheless, I refer the patient to the local doctor for joint treatment. However, that does not work in the case of malaria especially when a child has it, because malaria is not treatment by the local doctor because the local doctor believes the child is going to die no matter what is done.

Since the introduction of one change in Yanomami culture can create enormous consequence among the Yanomami, it is necessary to become an expert in their medical system before practicing in their area. For example, the use of needles has enormous consequences. When there are health problems, the ministry in Venezuela introduces needles. Yanomami take needles for everyone and unhappily this spreads diseases such as Hepatitis B rapidly.

A major factor in the health problems of the Yanomami is economic. There are relatively few Yanomami, about 23,000 total between Brazil and Venezuela. But it is costly to treat their problems and many Venezuelans object to spending money on people whom they consider primitive. A doctor is paid very little. When I went to the Yanomami in 1986 for the first time, my government salary was $2000 per year. Since the government has political pressures on its spending for Indians, we are forced to seek private donations.

But even preparing grants for private foundations is a problem. There are difficulties in getting the appropriate equipment to conduct the research or in controlling the taking and preservation of specimens. There are few epidemiologists willing to work in the conditions found in the Upper Orinoco area. There are competing demands for funds. There is always the problem of convincing people to invest in Indians who are perceived as contributing little to the overall good of Venezuela.

Thus, there are diseases that contribute to the death of the Yanomami. But there are also factors in the political economy of the country that limits our effectiveness in treating the diseases that threaten the Yanomami.

Student Questions

1. How does anthropology contribute to the practice of medicine among the Yanomami?

2. Why does Venezuela's politics work against the health of the Yanomami?

3. How do Western conceptions of health and disease conflict with Yanomami ideas?

4. How might an effective health program for the Yanomami be designed?

Chapter 5

Who Speaks for the Yanomami?
A New Tribe's Perspective

Greg Sanford

Much has been written and much has been said in the recent years concerning the Yanomami people who live in the Amazon junction of Venezuela and Brazil. For various reasons they have attracted the interest and attention of many people and groups. In these days of global interest in the Yanomami tribe, and with so much being written and said about them one wonders who, in reality, speaks for the Yanomami? This is a very good question.

Because of its cultural norms the Yanomami tribe has no political structure that can represent the tribe as a whole. Therefore, there are no real tribal spokesmen. Even on a village level the Yanomami don't have "Chiefs" as we know them from other tribes who have any real authority over the village. They have leaders who lead through example and by suggestion. However, the rest of the people only follow them if they want to, and in fact often they don't. There are numerous examples of young men who, through acts of aggression, have involved their village in a fight with another group, and alleged leaders of the village seem helpless to stop it.

Another reason that no real spokesmen exist from within the tribe is the fact that the Yanomami themselves don't think of their tribe as one unit. Most only know their own village and a few others that they occasionally visit or are at war with. Beyond that they really don't care. A Yanomami only cares about his immediate relatives, and he shows very little emotion or feeling about anyone else. There are no Yanomami who represent the whole tribe. When a Yanomami says he does represent the whole tribe, he is usually a product of outside influence from groups interested in the Yanomami, and, therefore, tends to represent the viewpoints of those groups. Because of this, the representation of the Yanomami tribe, up to this point, been very subjective, depending on who is the particular source of information. If through the information gathered in this book, we can obtain an unbiased report on what the actual situation among the Yanomami is, and find out in general what they want for their own future, this will be a major accomplishment.

Up until a few years ago, before the gold miners invaded the Yanomami areas in Brazil, the two main views on the Yanomami came from mission groups and anthropologists. Missionaries were accused by anthropologists of destroying the culture of the Indians, and only caring about converting the Indians, while anthropologists were accused of wanting to create zoological parks for the Indians, where we more advanced human beings could keep them for research purposes. Neither of these views is entirely true, even though there is some truth in the accusations from both sides. Some missionaries have not been considerate enough of Yanomami culture, and some anthropologists cared so much about the culture that they have tended to forget the Indians who live within the culture. It seems that in general missionaries care more about the people as individuals, whereas the anthropologists care more about the culture.

Let me give you an example. When I came to Venezuela on my first visit in 1972, I visited two very similar villages. In one, called Koshirowetheri, there was a house of an American evangelical missionary, and in the other, called Tayaritheri, there was small hut of a French Anthropologist. Both villages contained about a hundred people. Three years ago I learned that the village where the French anthropologist did his study has disappeared, because of warfare and sickness. I am not suggesting that it was the fault of the anthropologist nor am I trying to say that all the people in that village died. The village became too small to defend itself, and the rest of the occupants joined other villages. The village had been maintained "pure" culturally but the people had suffered greatly.

In the meantime, what had happened in the village where the American missionary worked? It had grown to over 300 people, one of the largest villages in the Yanomami tribe. Most of the increase was through reproduction, but a few people from other villages had joined them because they wanted the health and social benefits that they could receive from the missionary. In this village the Yanomami were no longer culturally "pure." They no longer practice shamanism nor the cultural dances. They don't give their young girls to be married to older men against their will, etc. There are even some cultural changes that I personally regret but the village continues to exist and prosper, and the people are alive and well.

Here in Parima "B", where I live, there were close to 250 Yanomami when New Tribes Mission started its work in 1968. Now in 1995 there are over 700 Yanomami even though more people have moved away from the valley than have moved in. This is because there are just too many people here now to support their traditional lifestyle. For the observer who may be worried about overpopulation, let me say that the increase in population is tapering off now that the people realize that most of their babies are going to live. In the earlier years of the mission work here, people continued their continual reproduction so as to maintain their numbers. This was very necessary in their former society where infant mortality was extremely high. But when the missionary arrived, with his medical help, most if not all babies made it into adulthood. This was something the Yanomami were not used to. As they have adapted to this help, the population has leveled out to a sustainable level. In many ways, it is good that there is an increase in population in parts of the Yanomami area because in other parts of their territory they are being devastated by warfare with guns as well as through sicknesses that they are not able to combat.

In some circles, the theory has been put forth with strong conviction that missionaries are really only concerned with converting the souls of the tribal people. Is this true? Are missionaries only concerned about converting the Yanomami? Nothing could be further from the truth. Although our main concern and our reason for coming here in the first place is the spiritual well being of the people, our work actually extends into many other areas. The two main areas are Education and Health. There are also other forms of Communal Development in which missionaries play a role.

A very large part of the missionary's time goes to caring for the medical needs of the Indians. In the earlier days of contact with the Yanomami tribe, it was exclusively the missionaries who did this type of work. Today though we are now working closely with the Venezuelan Government to train tribal people to do some medical work for themselves. Because of rough living conditions, medical doctors will rarely remain in Yanomami territory for very long. Because of this problem the best way to approach the need for medical workers among the Yanomami seems to be to have Yanomami medical workers take care of minor health problems while the more seriously ill are transported to far away hospitals by airplane.

Even though the Yanomami are still isolated in many ways, they are not isolated from disease. In the early to mid 1960s, a measles epidemic swept through the tribe, killing more than half the population in many villages. Hepatitis and malaria are present in every Yanomami region, killing hundreds of people every year. The Yanomami's lack of knowledge about disease, as well as their life-style, promote quick spread of most of these diseases. They share the same utensils for drinking; they share tobacco from each others' mouths; they share needles for digging out sand fleas; they live in open houses, unprotected from mosquitoes. Often they drink contaminated water, and children are allowed to play in contaminated mud around the houses. When they get sick, it is attributed to spirits or witches, and they try to avenge themselves on the people whom they blame. Therefore, their lack of medical knowledge and help leads them to level witchcraft charges against other innocent victims whom they then seek to kill in revenge for those who have died as a result of diseases.

In discussing development work among the Yanomami Tribe with those interested in the matter, many people have told me that in their opinion it would be best to educate the Yanomami about the source of diseases and how they can be cured without interfering in their religious beliefs. This is simply impossible. Once a Yanomami has learned about the source and cure for sickness, you have taken a way about 80% of his religion, because most of the Yanomami religious practices center around curing sick people, or protecting them from illnesses. At the present time, many promote a combination of modern medicine along with the traditional witchcraft. This is done out of respect for the culture.

Personally, I feel strongly that we are doing them a disservice, and really showing them disrespect by leaving them in the dark about the causes of death, and scientific knowledge concerning disease and sickness. Of course, education concerning disease, and its cause and cure should be done carefully and with sensitivity over a period of time, so as to not upset the balance within the society.

With regard to education, the only schools that exist in the Yanomami tribe are those established by Evangelical and Catholic missionaries. A New Tribes' missionary, James Barker, was the first to put the Yanomami language into writing and since then hundreds of Yanomami children have been taught to read. Realistically, the only way the Yanomami is going to be preserved, is when missionaries teach Yanomami children to read, and when missionaries produce written material in the Yanomami language. Our goal as evangelical missionaries is to create schools within the tribe that ultimately have Yanomami teachers working for the Venezuelan government who will carry on the work of education within their own area. What could be better then Yanomami teaching other Yanomami?

Because of the dedication of New Tribes Missionaries to the preservation of tribal people, their culture and customs, all of the work of New Tribes Mission is done in the Yanomami language. Because all our work has been done in their language, we believe that perhaps more than anyone else, we are helping to preserve the Yanomami.

As I traveled to different tribes in Venezuela recently, I saw group after group, where the children are no longer speaking their mother tongue. They go to school often away from their tribe, where only Spanish is spoken. The language and culture of several of these groups are on the verge of extinction. These are tribes where no missionaries are working. Missionary work in the tribal area gives tribal groups more of a pride in their own language and builds up a respect for that language in their own eyes. This is very important if we are to see groups like the Yanomami maintain their language and identity in the modern age.

Do missionaries and anthropologists have to work against each other even though we do have opposing viewpoints in certain areas? I do not feel that our roles should have to be adversarial. In days like these, when the Yanomami tribe is threatened from so many different angles, it is important that those parties who are truly interested in the well being of these people, work together in as many areas as possible. Missionaries and anthropologists actually can keep one another accountable, and by constructive criticism, we can help keep each other keep a balanced approach to our works.

Anthropology is indeed important to us missionaries. Each member of The New Tribes Mission is required to take an extensive course in Practical Anthropology before going into the field. In recent years we have been much more conscious of the importance of doing our work within the context of the tribal culture. We want to see the Yanomami maintain their cultural identity. We hope they never lose this identity and maintain the pride and joy in being Yanomami.

We also want to give the Yanomami an opportunity to learn the truth of the Bible. Those who make a personal decision to believe in Jesus Christ we teach to live according to Christian principles. In no way do we want to force or manipulate them into accepting our religion or the Bible. In fact the opposite is true. We try to guard against people following the teaching of the Bible for the wrong reasons, because this will only create confusion. We believe God knows the heart of man and God knows if a person's Christianity is coerced or whether it is from an inner conviction to follow Christ. I have many friends among the Yanomami who openly tell me they do not believe what we teach, and I completely respect their freedom to believe what they choose. They are still my friends!

Missionaries also help by promoting continuity in the contact between the Yanomami and the outside world. Anthropologists, doctors, teachers, soldiers, government workers, and others, come and go, while missionaries generally spend their whole lives living with the Indians. We develop personal hardships with them. They know us. Countless times we have been the bridge between them and doctors, government workers, soldiers, and, yes, even anthropologists. Recently a newly arrived doctor was going to help a young woman who was having trouble giving birth. He sent for me, saying that the woman and her mother wouldn't let him near her. I went down to the hut and spent five minutes reassuring them that what the doctor was going to do was necessary for the mother and the baby. After that the doctor had no problem doing his work, and the baby was safely delivered.

I have spent 19 years with the Yanomami. Some of them I call "brother, sister, uncles, mothers, grandmothers and grandfathers." Recently some of the children have started to call me "uncle" and even "grandfather." Some have known me from the day they were born. I have lived with them in their houses, traveled with them through the jungles, hunted and fished with them. I have laughed with them and I have cried with them. I have held some of my dead friends in my arms. I have spoon-fed some of them when they were on the verge of dying. I can count dozens of them who would have died if we hadn't been here. I have seen some, due to their faith in Jesus Christ, go from deep hatred for their enemies to love for them and showing compassion to them.

I have a hard time looking at the Yanomami people as "natives," "Indians," "aborigines" or whatever you may choose to call them. I see them as human beings, people who have the same emotions and feel as you and I. After all, the word Yanomami simply means "human being." Must we look at them as some kind of exotic beings that exist only to satisfy our curiosity? Instead of us outsiders always talking about them let us ask them what they think!

When I talk to the Yanomami about their concerns, there is one thing that always stands out in their minds, and that is, the concern for their physical health and concern for enough food to eat and feed their families. I recently had to meet with some of the leaders where I explained to them that this book was going to be written and that they would have the opportunity to tell the people on the outside what THEY wanted in the future. They were unanimous in saying that what they wanted the most was medicine, and for some of their men to learn to administer it. They also wanted schools, and tools for gardening, Some other things that were also important to them were cooking pots, knives, thread, fish hooks, matches and scissors. Apart from these concerns, they weren't very interested in the outside world.

Another thing that they said that surprised me, because I have always felt so welcomed by them is that they don't want many outsiders to come to live in their area. They have come to know enough outsiders to realize that most don't show real respect for them. They know that with increase in contact with the "outside," there is an increase in sickness. They are afraid of the advance of gold miners, so they want soldiers to be stationed here to stop them. They want doctors and missionaries to train them for a better future, but they don't want people to come who will take their land and treat them as inferiors.

So as we look down the road into the future of the Yanomami tribe, it would be very refreshing if missionaries, anthropologists and other groups interested in the promotion of the Yanomami tribe, could work together for their betterment. It would be much healthier if we could learn to treat them as people, not as a mere culture, and begin to realize that they are people just like ourselves that have the same desires that we do.

The Yanomami want a better life for their children, and they want medical help, so that will not lose their children when they are still two years old. They want the benefit of some of the conveniences that the outside world has, and they feel they have as much right to these things as any other person does. At the same time, they want to maintain their tribal lands and customs without the outside world forcing in on them with demands to change, or move. We need to respect their wishes and let them decide what they want and when they want it. And if their desire for some of the material goods that the outside world has to offer may cause some change in their culture, we as outsiders need to step back and let them decide what they want and how much change they want and respect their decisions!! For it is they who should decide such things, not we outsiders who may think we know what is best for the Yanomami!

Student Questions

1. What is the primary reason for the New Tribes Mission to be in Venezuela?

2. How does their work differ from that of anthropologists?

3. Why have missionaries and anthropologists clashed in New Tribes areas? Is this clash inevitable?

4. How may missionaries and anthropologists cooperate for the good of the Yanomami?

5. What contributions have the New Tribes made for the good of the Yanomami?

6. In your opinion, what has been the most important influence that the New Tribes Missionaries have had on the Yanomami?

7. Would teaching the Yanomami about modern medicine destroy Yanomami culture? If it would, should it be taught them anyway? Why?

8. What, according to the New Tribes Missionaries, do the Yanomami really want?

9. Why is it difficult to know who really speaks for the Yanomami, according to the New Tribes Missionaries?

10. What do *you* think about the ethics of changing a people's religion?

Chapter 6

The Missionary Effort to Help the Yanomami Speak for Themselves

Padre Jose Bortoli

I am happy to address people who have an interest in the Yanomami and consider them important and relevant in terms of the world situation. In regard to the question that Professor Salamone proposed, "Who Speaks for the Yanomami?", all of us are in agreement that the goal in all of this is that the Yanomami speak for themselves. Enabling the Yanomami to speak for themselves is the goal of the educational process which the Salesians have initiated among the Yanomami. The primary goal of the Salesians in our educational program and in all our work has been to bring the Yanomami to the point where they are able to speak for themselves. Emergency cases arise, however, in which action needs to be taken quickly and in which other people have to enter into the situation beside the Yanomami themselves and talk about the situation.

Problems really begin when the Yanomami themselves begin to speak. Currently, a demagogic situation exists in which once a Yanomami starts speaking, everyone starts to applaud what he said simply because a Yanomami has spoken. Even if others may not be in favor of what is said by a fellow Yanomami, they will applaud simply because one of their own has spoken to people in power.

The sad aspect of this understandable chauvinism is that often they lose sight of their own true interests in presenting a united front against the outside world.

There is a great necessity to enter into a dialogue with the Yanomami, to realize that the Yanomami are capable of dialogue, and in the dialogue to begin to understand that there is no single Yanomami position or problem. There are, as among other peoples, many problems and many positions. A major issue often forgotten is to whom should the Yanomami be speaking?

I admire Professor Chagnon because he took a whole day to explain to a simple Padre the position of sociobiology. I admire these qualities of dialogue. I agree that the problems which Professor Chagnon has outlined in his presentation are indeed the real problems of the Yanomami. I am in complete agreement on this point. However, in the dispute which has arisen between the Salesians and Chagnon, I want to understand in the sense of dialogue the positions which have been taken in order to remedy the situation.

I think that one of the fundamental problems was a supposition or assumption on the part of Professor Chagnon that the Salesians were the only cultural brokers between the Yanomami or the cultural leader of speakers between the Yanomami and the outside world. I am in complete agreement with Professor Chagnon that the main question here is the interest of the Yanomami themselves and that we must put aside these controversies of the past in order to meet the problems that Professor Chagnon has outlined.

I wish to state that there are many other speakers between the Yanomami and the outside world in addition to the Salesians. The health service which is concerned with malaria, for example, has a large number of people who are intermediaries between the Yanomami and the outside world. There are a lot of people who aid and represent Yanomami interests besides missionaries: the Environmental Commission, Educational Ministry, the Health Ministry, soldiers - even anthropologists .

And one must realize and remember one thing. I wish to emphasize this point. The presence of the Salesians missionaries has guaranteed a continuity of presence of these intermediate speakers. This presence is very important because when crisis

situations arise, it is necessary that personnel be on the scene
immediately and react to it immediately in order to try to alleviate
the situation. If one must wait to call in a specialist, an
anthropologist or whatever it may be, the loss of time means that
you lose the battle.

For example, there is problem of the creation of the Yanomami
park. There is also the question of where the military wishes to
establish posts within the Yanomami area. Moreover, there is the
problem of the division of the Yanomami territory in terms of the
administration of the territory. The establishment of the Yanomami
park along the lines first proposed, for instance, would have created
a division within the Yanomami territory itself because it would
have created a division among Yanomami who are within the proposed park territory, as I understand it, as opposed to the
Yanomami who were not within the park territory. However, the
presence of the missionaries guaranteed a dialogue that remained
focused on the terms of the situation . It guaranteed that the
dialogue is was carried on against the background of the realities of
the situation itself.

One of the difficulties is that many of the anthropologists who
deal with the territory are quite unaware of the wider political
context of Venezuela itself which, of course, is having an impact on
the Yanomami. And that they are also unaware of the context of
the anthropological world of the Venezuelans themselves. And as
a result, when any anthropologists come in from outside of
Venezuela into these questions, it is very important that you understand the national context. Both the political context of the nation
itself, as well as the context of the national anthropological group
that is working within the country.

I thinks that the problem that arose between the Salesians and
Professor Chagnon was a political type of problem. I sincerely can
say that the Salesians never opposed the work of Chagnon among
the Yanomami. That just prior to the outbreak of the controversy,
there was a common project between the Salesians and Professor
Chagnon in regard to genealogical work, in regard to the naming
system. And that prior to this there had been a number of instances
of cooperation between the Salesians and Professor Chagnon.

There was a project on Funda Fosi and the Salesians were in
opposition to this program and Professor Chagnon evidently was

involved in this program. However, we Salesians believed that Professor Chagnon at that time was unaware of some of the wider political implications of this project. In regard to this project, the Salesians and the Bishop of the area were in disagreement. The Bishop, a Salesian himself, was in favor of the project; the Salesians missionaries in the field were against the project. So, again, this is the problem of the wider context that must be understood. If anyone wishes to know more about that situation, you simply have to dig into the concrete facts in the total context of the situation.

The problem of health is indeed the primary problem for the Yanomami. I am in complete agreement with Professor Chagnon. The problem of internal warfare among the Yanomami is also very serious. The accusation that the Salesians are partially responsible for some of the mortality because of some of our work there is a very delicate issue. I understand Chagnon's position but I do not agree with it. But we can leave it as something in the past.

It is true that we are also there to evangelize or, better, to bear witness, but at the very moment I realize my evangelization is leading to destruction of the Yanomami, of its culture, of its social economic systems at this moment I would certainly question my work in evangelization. One of the most difficult problems for us is that there is another church group, The New Tribes Missions that is violating, according to the Salesian view, the human rights of the Yanomami. For example, they are prohibiting the performance of traditional funeral rites. They are doing away with the traditional funeral system of the Yanomami. For us there is the basic principle that all cultures are from God. For The New Tribes Missions these different cultural forms, including those of the Yanomami, are the work of the devil. The theological position of the Salesians is that the Gospel can be adapted to all cultures and can be a revitalization force for all cultures.

The Yanomami Park

In 1977 the Venezuelan government made some efforts to create a national park within the Yanomamo territory. Well as things usually happen, as affairs happen in Venezuela, wait for the unexpected. There were two proposals that were being aired and

while these were in discussion the government was changed and
both of them ended up in the garbage. In 1979 there was a meeting
in Caracas in which Yanomami, missionaries, anthropologists and
other interested individuals participated. The object was to create
a Yanomami territory.

The possibility exists of creating areas within the country under
a special regime. But on the other hand there are limitations. For
example the concept of *ethnia* (ethnic identity) does not exist.
Perhaps, it is better to say that it exists in potential, but it has not
been activated. The concept of a group, an indigenous people, was
not discussed. Therefore, the only topic discussed were criteria that
could be used to create a Yanomami territory. The most important
point, given the Brazilian experience where the Yanomami group
was divided and dispersed among different areas, was to create one
continuous territory. Another crucial factor was to insist on the
participation of the Yanomami in the creation of their own territory. The creation of a Yanomami territory in Brazil was the
object of interminable discussions and people were continually
taking steps backward instead of forward. Miraculously in Venezuela
the creation of a territory occurred within a one month period.

The only concept that could be used legally was the concept of
a park because there is a very important park service throughout the
country. So the concept of park and the notion of peoples, any
peoples, living within the park already existed. Perhaps the park was
not as large for example as various groups would have liked, but in
any case they managed to create one. And people like Napoleon
Chagnon were also asked for their advice, and I believe that
Napoleon Chagnon spoke to the president at the time, and the
project was pushed through very quickly.

Outside people can stay within the park and sometimes they
even have ownership of pieces of land within the park, but they are
under the jurisdiction of a number of rules and regulations. In any
case that was the most appropriate and best concept that they had
available for them, the concepts of the park. We not only tried to
analyze the ecological aspect but the presence of the Yanomami and
the entire territory and trying to create concepts and rules that later
on could not be changed, once they were incorporated into this
concept of park. Once and for all it was clear that the Yanomami
were the original inhabitants of this habitat. It could, for example,

insist that they only move within certain areas, they were to have the free range of the entire territory. They had the complete right to participate in their traditional economic activity although there may be certain restrictions to the intensity of that activity. They could even develop new projects within their territory, even non-traditional projects, but these must be considered sustainable.

We took advantage of the fact that this was the year of the Brazilian conference and the president had these issues at hand and to everybody's amazement the project was approved in less than a month, even before Brazil's. For your knowledge, at this very moment (December 2, 1994), the Yanomami are having a conference, or a reunion, within their own territory to establish the regulations of the use of the territory. We want to do away with the old fashioned concept of parks where people are told from the outside, "this is what you can do and this is what you cannot do." The park was created with the concept of "no, let's not create the park first and then we'll see what we'll do with the population that's within it," but for there to be a truly dynamic relationship between the indigenous peoples within the park and their ambient.

Now that we have defined the Yanomami vis-a-vis their territory, we are in the process of determining what sort of rules will exist in regard to people who come in from the outside. For example, tourists. But the most crucial factor of this entire discussion is the importance of the participation of the Yanomami in their own future.

There are rules, laws, regarding the creation of biospheres. And paradoxically more activity can be permitted within a biosphere, such as mining, in comparison to a national park. Another activity that can be permitted is the colonization projects. This is the reason why we wanted to create a park and not a biosphere. Not only that but we want a park for historical reasons. Because in future generations and in future times everybody will know that the park is synonymous with the Yanomami territory. We all know that the concept of territory, and everybody has a right to know, that this is the Yanomami territory. Not only the place where they are or the land that they use, but their territory.

There are certain restrictions in regard to the park, regarding people and projects that come from the outside. The last remaining problem is the concept of property. And to my knowledge this has not been obtained in Brazil either. The park is part of the Venezuelan nation and therefore Venezuelan authorities like the national guard and the army have an obligation to protect the territory.

Conclusion

The answer to the question of who speaks for the Yanomami is, of course, that the Yanomami should speak for themselves. In today's world, however, that is not always feasible. Our job as Salesian missionaries has been to establish bilingual schools, in Spanish and Yanomami, to train the Yanomami to be heard and to represent their own interests. We have tried to build up a sense of ethnic identity among them so that they will unite as one people among many others. We do not wish to substitute warfare of the Yanomami against outsiders for internal warfare.

The Yanomami are an endangered people as recent attacks against them by illegal Brazilian miners has demonstrated. They need the protection of the Venezuelan army and National Guard. We have fought for the Yanomami Park so that the Yanomami will have their own territory within Venezuela, a territory they can develop in conformity with their own beliefs and traditions.

Only when they are seen by others as a people worthy of respect and dignity will they be able to speak as equals within a multicultural Venezuela. Learning Spanish, speaking in modern democratic forums, attending schools, running their own cooperative and developing their own projects will bring about changes in the Yanomami. As they themselves note, however, they have the right to change as much as any anthropologist does. So long as these changes do not affect their self-identity, they will remain Yanomami. The option is not between changing and not-changing. It is between change in conformity with their traditions or death - physical and cultural extinction.

Student Questions

1. Why is it difficult to find any Yanomami who speaks for all Yanomami?

2. What does Padre Bortoli view as the work of the Salesian missionaries among the Yanomami?

3. What is the Yanomami Park? What are its advantages and disadvantages?

4. What does Padre Bortoli mean when he states that the problems between Chagnon and the Salesians were political problems?

5. What differences exist between the New Tribes and the Salesian missions?

6. In what manner is anthropology important for the Salesian missionaries according to Bortoli?

7. What benefits, according to Bortoli, have the Salesians brought to the Yanomami?

8. If Bortoli's main work is not conversion, in what way is he a missionary?

9. Can the Salesians be accused of paternalism? Why?

10. In what ways do the Salesians attempt to ascertain Yanomami views on development?

Chapter 7

The Yanomami Speak for Themselves

Frank A. Salamone, Based on Statements from Yanomami Residing Near the New Tribes and Salesian Missions in Venezuela on the Upper Orinico River

The Yanomami are perfectly capable of speaking for themselves. They do so daily and with great eloquence. The problem lies in our not being able to hear them since their speeches are given in areas remote from our daily experiences. Their voices, moreover, are often drowned out by the din that others who profess to speak for them make. Therefore, I collected statements from the Yanomami at Salesian mission stations on issues they deem important. Greg Sanford collected statements on similar issues from Yanomami at New Tribes stations.

Although the Yanomami do not present a "united front," they do show a remarkable similarity on essential issues: land, development, the role of missionaries, medical needs, and so forth. This similarity of opinion is remarkable among a group that does not have central leadership and whom all reliable commentators portray as "rugged individualists." Individualists they indeed are, but the essential problems of the Yanomami are clear in areas of contact between the Yanomami and outsiders who threaten their lives.

Thus, although the Yanomami have no special mystical with their land, recent difficulties have made them acutely aware of the need to take steps to protect their claims to the land. There is no difference among those who reside near the New Tribes or the Salesians on this issue. Tomasito who resides near the New Tribes states matters in this way:

> In the beginning we didn't think about protecting our land, but after I heard that outsiders had taken the land of Indians down river, I started to think that we need to protect our land. I have told everybody that we don't want others to live on our land. I also don't want tourists to come. I am not against the Catholic missionaries coming, but because they bring other Yanomami with them that want to be over us, I am not asking them to come. In the beginning when the outsiders first started to come, my elders didn't think this way, but now my brother and I think this way. We have started to write letters to the Government and the Army to tell them about the gold miners, so that they can chase them away. I don't want the soldiers to live, but it is necessary so that the Gold miners won't steal our land.

Yanomami who reside along the Orinoco near the Salesian stations also have become protective of their lands and routinely ask visitors to show them their "papers," allowing them to be in their area. These government permits are not easy to obtain, and I was happy to show them at each village when asked. The Yanomam with whom I spoke pointed out that they did not wish to offend me as a visitor but had to protect themselves given current conditions. These conditions included the then recent slaughter of Yanomami by illegal gold miners.

The fact that I was in the company of Salesian missionaries made my welcome easier. It is interesting to note the Yanomami evaluation of missionaries. Rarely do the Yanomami mention the missionaries without mentioning what they do for them. Their evaluation has an openly utilitarian ring to it.

> We need to have some of us become health workers, while others plant gardens, so that we can live well. The missionaries teach us. They have been teaching us for a long time. Some of us have become Christians and some of us haven't. but they help us anyway. Some of us need to become health workers, so that when the missionaries go, we will be able to get medical help. If we don't think

like that, other outsiders will come here and live, and they will decide over us. Let us think really well before the missionaries go, so that others won't come after them and take our land away from us. Some of us need to become teachers, some need to become medical workers. I want to represent our people to the outside, even though I don't know a lot of Spanish yet (Tomasito).

Yanomami near the Salesian stations offer similar evaluations of missionaries but with a bite more typical of Yanomami. They remember Padre Coco who was a very generous man. The newer missionaries strive to reduce Yanomami dependency and therefore would rather teach skills than pass out food or money. Yanomami evaluations are rather tart but fair.

We are content with the missionaries. The missionaries have done good things for us but the new missionaries are cheap. They are not generous like Father Coco. They don't give us things like he did. They always tell us to work, to plan. We think it is better to be generous and to give things. But they are good men. They have built schools and they tell us not to fight to settle our problems in peace. To protect ourselves from outsiders who bring sickness and who come to kill us.

The Yanomami attitude toward the missions is interesting given the attacks some anthropologists have made at one time or another. I specifically asked Yanomami near the Salesian station what their evaluation was of Napoleon Chagnon's attacks. These Yanomami had heard of the attacks through the Salesians and had been shown articles from Venezuelan papers. Since there are Spanish speaking Yanomami and Yanomami teachers, it is not surprising that they keep up with the news as it relates to their interests. Granted that those who profit from the Salesians' presence would be more favorably disposed to their cause. Nevertheless, the opinion of these pro-mission Yanomami is interesting. One Yanomami responded to the charge that missionaries incite Yanomami to fight in this fashion:

The Yanomami laugh at the idea that anyone could claim that the missionaries ask us to fight. The missionaries are always telling us to stop fighting and live in peace, to settle our disputes peacefully. Magic is a more important cause of fighting than women. When someone goes to a Shabono and blows on the people causing harm, then there is war.

Another Yanomami walked in while I was interviewing people. He thought I was accusing missionaries of giving them shotguns, one of Chagnon's charges against the Salesians. His response was immediate and vehement:

> You are liars. The mission never gave us shotguns. Why are you strangers such liars? The missionaries never sent us to kill Chagnon. There is no case of Yanomami hurting whites.

Alberto [*...handwritten note: "Internal controversy - trag. grads"...*] nts, agrees with other Yanomami [...] them to kill Chagnon. "The missio[...] ," say the Yanomami. Alberto say[...] er the missions spoke bad about h[...] they did not. He told him that the [...] d about him. Alberto says that wh[...] on's colleague, interviewed him, [...] and Brewer Carias said that he said that Alberto stated that the missionaries said they wanted Yanomami to kill Chagnon. According to Alberto, Chagnon was not there. Brewer Carias alone was there. Chagnon thinks that the missions prevent him from doing research among the Yanomami.

Alberto walks a fine line between his loyalty to Chagnon and the missions. He defends Chagnon from mission charges of purposely blowing a roof off a shabono, a Yanomami dwelling.

> It is not true that Chagnon blew away a Shabono on purpose. He landed in the middle of the Shabono. It was Kiomithatheri. When he landed they wanted to blow up the helicopter. Because I, Alberto, told them not to land the helicopter. The Yanomami were prohibiting landing because they think strangers will bring illness - malaria, measles . The missions discuss these problems with them.

It was this incident that seems to be the basis of Chagnon's charge that missionaries are keeping him out of the Amazon, or stirring up the Yanomami to do so. Certainly, there was a great deal of Salesian antagonism toward Chagnon.

At Mavaquita I gathered this statement:

We don't get guns from missions. We work and trade and go to
Puerto Ayacucho for them. Chagnon is lying, *nasi*. We have five
guns and bought them in Puerto Ayacucho. Chagnon is lying. Shaki
is very *nasi* because he doesn't like missionaries. Chagnon wants to
be here alone. To send away the missionaries. Three guns came
from Brazilian Yanomami. Now we don't fight anywhere. We have
schools. We only shoot animals, not people.

This theme of fighting less and concentrating on development
is echoed among the New Tribes Yanomami. They state that they
need to stop fighting and hating each other. In common with the
Salesian Yanomami they assert that they already fight less then they
did and need to continue to decrease their fighting. The Yanomami
who live near mission stations agree that the missions have sought
to bring peace. There is also a greater awareness of the need to
work together and protect their land.

Some of our people want outsiders to come here so that they will
get free food from them, but I don't want that! At first maybe they
will give out free food but later they will start fencing in the land
and tell us to go and live somewhere else. This is our land, not
land for the outsiders to live on. I don't more outsiders to come to
live here. This is our land, not outsiders' land.

The things that the Yanomami state they want are rather simple,
perhaps, but they essential to preserving and enhancing their way of
live. They want machetes and axes for gardens. They state that they
don't ask for clothes because "I am an Indian, and therefore don't
have to wear clothes." What they want is equally as revealing as
what they do want. As Enrique states:

I don't want people from the outside to come and live here. I don't
want them to take our land. After they have taken our land, where
are we going to live? There is no other good land for gardening.
Why do I want the Military to live here? It is because people fight.
it is because they take women by force. That is why I wanted them
to come. I said: 'Send the military here so that we 'll not fight
among each other.' That's what I said, and that's why they are
here. I don't want any other outsiders to live here.

This desire to keep outsiders away, however, does not appear to extend to the missionaries. Granted, some Yanomami at both stations argue that the missionaries are too selfish in sharing their possessions. But they admit that no one, including the Yanomami, really likes to share everything either. Moreover there is a fear that when missionaries leave, they will leave a real gap. The Yanomami worry that the will not have a ready source for medicine without a missionary presence. Without medicine many of the children will die, and even the adults will die.

> Because I think that I want medicine. I want medicine for all kids of diseases. Even if I have a lot of things. I can still die. Because of that I am not saying that I want a lot of things. I just want machetes and axes. When we don't have those we don't have food to eat. Because of that I want those. I also want a machine to grind manioc roots. I won't get any help from just having things. Because of that I am not saying that I want outsiders to live there that will give us a lot of things. No, I don't want them to come to live here. I don't want any other outsiders to live here. When the military came they started to hand out rice and sardines. Because of that some say: "Let us tell the missionaries to go home! They don't give us food." No! I don't say that. I want to have the missionaries to teach us. There are a lot of things that we don't know yet. When they have finished teaching us, and when they want to, they cam go home.

This last phrase is a prime example of Yanomami realism. There is no sentimentality nor attempt to hide the pragmatism in their relationship with missionaries.

The missionaries have made the Yanomami conscious of western medicine. There are many statements in the interviews regarding the need to improve and take control of the health care system. The Yanomami are clear that they desire more Yanomami to become health workers. Too many doctors come and go because of the hard conditions in the Amazon. Moreover, they want Yanomami lab technicians "to read the microscopes for parasites." Others need to give out medicine as infirmarians. They are well aware that if there is only one health workers and he dies, then they are in trouble.

"There needs to be many health workers. so that when one quits there will be others to take his place."

They are aware that you cannot always "see" what disease people have. That is why, they say, they want their own people to study how to see in microscopes. "That is why one of our young men, Elisea, is taking a course in using microscopes, to see if people have malaria." They state that it is good to have people go to learn to take care of the people. They are clear that want Yanomami doctors and that the Yanomami will learn medicine easily. The New Tribes Yanomami offer the example of a man named Antonio who lived close to them:

We suffered a lot from diseases, but he helped us with medicine. With that he make the sickness go away. Don't think that in the beginning we didn't suffer from sickness. The older ones sure remember. Now we are protected by the medicine. Because we think that, we want medicine. When we suffer from sickness, the missionaries send for medicine. They help us. They are our friends, and we are also their friends. Even though they come from a different place, they came to live among us. Living among us they helped us. The missionaries that teach God's word, I am not sending them away. That word is good. Others are saying: "Just let them live the way they used to! 'No, I don't live well. I cried a lot. Did the sickness start when the missionaries came? No! Before the missionaries came, there was a lot of sickness. We already suffered a lot. Before we weren't many, but now we have a lot of children. Why is that? It is because of the medicine. Because of medicine we increased. It is because of it that we are alive. If the missionaries hadn't come, the few of us that lived would have died and there wouldn't have been anyone left. It was not good when we were at war. The ones that say that we should continue to fight the way we used to, they lie. No! When we fight we go hungry. We are constantly on the watch out for the enemy, and because of that can't garden. No! The ones that say that the missionaries just deceive us, and want us to live the way we used to, they are the ones that are lying. 'Just let them go on dying the way they used to!', that is what they are saying. 'Just let them go on hurting one another'; that is what they say. Even though they know God's word they go on saying that.

This long quote is typical of the manner in which the mission Yanomami circle back to the discussion on whether the missionaries should stay or go and whether they have been good for the Yanomami. The frequent quotes of what other Yanomami say is clear evidence of the manner in which Yanomami have pondered the issue. There is a clearly evidence that the Yanomami think that missionaries will go someday. They want to ensure that before that happens they are able to do what the missionaries do in terms of medicine, schooling, and technology. There is also evidence that the missionaries have been the least harmful of any of the outsiders. They certainly have not taken Yanomami women, nor stolen their land, nor killed them.

As another Yanomami states if they want to be sure that strangers stay away they have to learn to be able to take of themselves in this modern world. Some Yanomami need to become health workers. Others must become schoolteachers. Still others have to become storekeepers. Yet others can cut boards with chain saws. While more can raise chickens or pigs. In spite of those who say that it is never going to be like that he feels that the Yanomami must really make an effort to turn this dream into reality. Isalito points out that the Yanomami who live down by the big rivers have succeeded in doing this, and they have motors and guns. These Yanomami have talked to people from the government, and the government people have given them machetes and shovels, seeds and poison to kill cockroaches. This teacher continues:

> What are the things that we want to have? When I start working as a teacher I wanted to get thread for tying arrows, and red cotton thread for making hammocks. Some of us want shorts, shoes, pants, hats, watches, fish hooks, matches, combs. In order to get these things we want to work. What things do I want? Because our skin itches a lot when we are dirty, we want soap to wash ourselves.

These items again strike me in their simplicity and usefulness. These are things the Yanomami can obtain for themselves, as they are quick to indicate.

Not everyone is opposed to having people from outside come to the Yanomami. A visitor from a village without contact with outside world was quite open in stating that he wanted people from the outside to come to his place. He said that he also wanted to get things from the outside. He would go so far as to build an airstrip so that outsiders will come to his village.

This eagerness to meet with outsiders has been part of Yanomami history. They have had a long history of trade with people who come through the Amazon. To repeat, it has only been relatively recent disasters that have made them careful of strangers. It is interesting to contrast this visitor's eagerness to build an airstrip, similar to the one at Mavaca, to bring the outside world to him with the caution shown, at least initially, by those who have had regular contact with the outside world. Although I must state that the Yanomami were unfailingly kind and, yes, even gentle in their dealings with me even though I had little material goods to trade and fewer skills to share in my brief visit.

One Yanomami stated this wariness regarding outsiders by opposing a Government road through his area. He feared that outsiders would prove unfriendly. "If a lot of them come to live here, they will fight with us and take our women. They will make us suffer." Reflecting, perhaps, on past experiences he stated that at first they would give food. That would lead to dependency, for "we will quit making gardens, and then we will really suffer." He indicated the need to learn how to make things for themselves without becoming dependent. Certainly, the common message of the Salesians and New Tribes missionaries seemed to get through to many; namely, it is necessary to learn skills and not take handouts. The handouts only lead to eventual suffering.

This lesson explains the generally favorable attitude to the military whom the Yanomami regard as their protection from illegal miners. They believe that the military came to protect the area. They further argue that if the military do not protect the area, the gold miners will poison the rivers and they will die.

The Yanomami also want the military to serve as outsiders to teach things that the missionaries will not or cannot teach. "Because the missionaries are always so busy translating and teaching the Bible, we want somebody else to teach us other things." Still they insist that they do not want other outsiders, other than the military and the missionaries, to come to their area to live. Here their worry about guns comes to the fore. They are sure that these outsiders will bring guns. They may not do so at first. Eventually, however, they will do so. However, they Yanomami admit that they get into fights too easily. "What is happening down river? They are fighting each

other with guns. Because of that I don't want guns to be brought
in." However, in a priceless switch, this Yanomami states, "Maybe
after a long time I will eventually get one gun. We should just have
one gun. Because there are so few animals in the jungle here, we
suffer. When they rains start and the tracks are easily seen, we will
got out to get some animals so that we can have our feasts. We
shouldn't have a lot, I just one. They we can lend it among
ourselves when we go hunting for a feast."

Yanomami ambivalence about guns is clear in this statement.
There is no doubt that guns are useful in hunting. There is also no
doubt that they help kill off game in a pattern too familiar in the
anthropological record. Moreover, guns are being used in warfare
and leading to increased mortality. It was Chagnon's charge that the
Salesians were making guns available to the Yanomami that heated
up their dispute. It is not illegal for any Venezuelan citizen to have
a gun. The Yanomami, as citizens, can use guns for hunting. However, behind the charge was the implication that the Salesians aided
the Yanomami who lived near their mission stations in their wars
against other Yanomami.

The Salesians have turned the argument around. They claim that
it is Chagnon who brought weapons to the Yanomami. Alberto,
Chagnon's assistant who was living at the mission stations states "I
went on an expedition to a far Shabono with Chagnon. Chagnon
picked up two *garampeiros*, illegal miners, in Brazil. The same
shotguns are here but are not Venezuelan. The Yanomami know
the difference between Brazilian and Venezuelan pots and pans and
machetes."

In an inventory of guns near a Salesian station a Yanomami
stated "We have some guns. We got one from Brazil; two from
Puerto Ayacucho; four from other Yanomami; one from L'
Esmeralda; one from the cooperative, Suajo. They are all old and
broken down. The missions have not agreed to sell guns to the
Yanomami. They forced Suajo to stop selling guns, even though
Suajo's gun came from a Venezuelan Assessor. It is not illegal for
Yanomami or any other Venezuelan citizen to have a gun for
peaceful purposes in the forest." It is that one gun sold by
Yanomami to Yanomami at the cooperative on mission lands that
is the source of the claim that the Salesians sell weapons to the

Yanomami. On the other hand, there is no doubt that such weapons are used in warfare.

The Yanomami who live near the Salesians, however, are clear that they do not believe that the missionaries sent them to war. On the contrary, they tried to stop them. They state that they always tell them to stop fighting. For example, there was a war in the area when I was there in November 1994. Six people were killed. Many fled to the mission station where they knew no one would attack them. Cesar, the man whom Chagnon states tried to kill him, said that he tried to kill only the killer. "Unfortunately, we killed some others." Cesar continues that he never had any intention of killing Chagnon. "I do not want to kill him. I may have to kill people but I am not a murderer. I long for the days of peace to come. Sometimes killing is necessary or you will die. But I am not a murderer."

There is another way that missionaries are said to be guilty of killing, that is by "killing with kindness." Yanomami at both mission areas state that this charge is a lie, *nasi*. They argue that missionaries help them. Sick Yanomami get medicine. Missionaries brought a school and a Coop. That state that "We Yanomami are poor men. We have to exchange." Moreover, the Mission transports ill people to doctor, as an infirmario in Mavaca notes. Moreover, the Yanomami note that the good that the coop and mission put in trading is not bad. These bring nets and tools for farming. Missionaries fight malaria. "When mosquitoes come, we wear shirts to keep them away. We learned this from the missionaries but missionaries do not tell us to put clothes on." Yanomami assert that they wear clothes when it makes sense to them. Wearing clothes does not make them less "authentic" nor does going nude make them more so.

The Yanomami at mission stations have some decided opinions about anthropologists. These, however, are quite sophisticated and distinguish between one anthropologist and another. The Salesian Yanomami, for example, took a great liking to Tim Asch, the anthropological film maker. Asch filmed Yanomami Indians. He showed his film to students in anthropology. He found out that students' response was not good. Asch, worried about this response, asked the Yanomami to view the film and comment on it. Yanomami noted that the film was accurate but asked Asch not to show it to whites because whites laugh at it. This consultation helped endear Asch to the Yanomami.

He also kept a promise to them to train them in taking films. He obtained a grant to do so and brought 8 mm video cameras to the Amazon. The Yanomami now make their own documentaries. "The School Is My Home" is their first. They also filmed the National Geographic unit that made a documentary on a Yanomami woman, Yarima, who married the anthropologist Ken Goode. They want to make films depicting Yanomami life today.

Perhaps doing so would avoid a recent incident that involved one of the Yanomami who was at a hospital in Puerto Ayacucho when the Yanomami were on TV. Other patients viewed the film and one of them made the mistake of laughing at the film. The Yanomami patient hit him. Yanomami state that non-Yanomami don't understand the meaning of what they see in these films and laugh. "Therefore, we don't want these films shown to whites. No one likes to have his way of life mocked." The main reason, however, that the Yanomami don't like to have their pictures taken is cultural. They state that they feel that the pictures take away part of their souls. This is especially true with small kids and those who are already ill. Taking pictures might make the small kids ill. However, a number of people sought me out to take their pictures. In fact, a number of people took my picture rather freely and I drew laughs when I noted that they were stealing my soul.

Attitudes vary. One Shabono didn't allow us to take their photos but I think they would have if approached more slowly. Another, at Platanal, allowed filming of the town meeting but kept the ill out of range. Of course, Padre Bortoli did the actual taping there. Some Yanomami in school have changed. They use pictures as trade items. They will pose for money or goods. However, some have gone to the ethnographic museum in Puerto Ayacucho and torn the faces off the photo exhibits there. Polaroids, however, make a difference. However, individual Yanomami takes pictures of friends just as we do.

On the other hand, a number of other Yanomami state that Chagnon's films, blood samples, photos of the dead annoy them.

He is always interested in taking pictures of vaginas. He violates taboos about speaking of the dead. Chagnon and his photos! I am tired of hearing tales of Chagnon speaking bad of missionaries. We don't want photos. We want Chagnon to stop speaking. We never heard tales about the missions trying to kill Chagnon.

In all fairness it must be added that one of the Yanomami present who complained of Chagnon's pictures violating taboos, muttered "and he pays so little, too." This statement caused Padre Bortoli to laugh and to warn me not to take their complaints about Chagnon too seriously.

It was here, Warapanatheri village, that Chagnon visited with his helicopter that blew the roof off the Shabono. The Yanomami who were complaining about him state that "We were afraid of garampeioros and that was why we were so fierce. Not because of missionaries." They stated that they would not have killed him. There were about thirty people there, and each assented to this speech. Another raised his hand to speak and stated that when the Yanomami fight, they do not fight every day. Furthermore, they fight for Yanomami custom not because of the missions tell them to fight. In fact, "they tell us not to fight."

Finally, what do the Yanomami say when they speak for themselves? They say that they do not want to be anybody's pet. They are tired of people taking advantage of them.

When the Border Commission was here they were really generous. They were giving out free food, and people would sit by their place every night after day, waiting for food. If the rest want to live like that just let them, but I don't want to live like that. I don't want us to be somebody's pets. The things that we want are these: Medicine, machetes, axes, matches, Nucca graters so that we can make manioc flour and cassava. We also want animals, so that we can have meat. like pigs and cows.

Moreover, the Yanomami do not want tourists whom they would entertain. They do not want to dance for them or perform "witchcraft." They do not want to be in a zoo or museum for the edification of others. "No, we don't want the people who say that to live with us." They want people who understand them, like the missionaries, and who teach them to care for themselves and survive in the modern world. That means education, medicine, and basic agricultural tools. Although "some don't want to study for those that want to, we need to let them." Moreover, it is important that some

Yanomami learn Spanish so that they can communicate with people from the outside and defend themselves. Some Yanomami should become teachers while others should become health workers, "so that we will live well anyway."

Many of the New Tribes Yanomami state eloquently that they want to be good Christians. It is interesting that none of the Salesian Yanomami state similar sentiments. In fact, Bortoli notes that he has no converts at his station. That is not his reason for being there. Nevertheless, the statements of the New Tribes Yanomami can not be dismissed out of hand. Certainly, they appear sincere and recognize a tie between what they want and the missionaries who enabled them to make notable progress toward that goal.

The Yanomami, in common with other endangered peoples, speak eloquently for themselves. Certainly, there is no one Yanomami opinion any more than there is one American opinion. Nevertheless, there is broad agreement among the Yanomami about their right to live their own lives and to obtain education, medicine, and peace. Those who seek to aid the Yanomami cannot ignore their opinions and judgments.

Student Questions

1. What do the Yanomami want from the outside world?

2. Why are they so suspicious of outsiders?

3. Which outsiders do they appear to welcome? Why?

4. Judging from Yanomami statements, discuss basic Yanomami characteristics.

5. What is the Yanomami evaluation of missionaries?

6. What does the charge that the missionaries are "killing the Yanomami with kindness" imply?

7. What do the Yanomami think of anthropologists?

8. Evaluate and discuss the Yanomami attitude toward film.

9. Why are some Yanomami afraid of becoming "pets" ? What does this expression mean in terms of the Yanomami's experience?

10. What does dependency mean in development terms? Why do development agents try to avoid creating dependency in populations undergoing development?

Chapter 8

The Yanomami Intercultural Schools

Frank A. Salamone

Yanomami Schools

In Amazonas State, Venezuela, all schools outside Puerto Ayacucho are Salesian. All but the Yanomami schools are boarding schools. After a disastrous attempt to send Yanomami boys to boarding schools in the 1960s at L'Esmeralda, the Salesians decided that "Boarding schools are not in the Yanomami 'mentality'," as Bishop Ignazio Velasco puts it. The Yanomami schools are within the Shabonos, Yanomami communal dwellings, and scattered.

Salesians founded schools from the start of the missions in 1957. In the 1960s they began introducing intercultural aspects in these schools but these were not well-organized. Three of these earlier missionaries were very supportive but lacked the knowledge and facility to organize an intercultural school system in the Amazon. At the Platanal mission outpost, creole and Yanomami attended school together. This was part of Padre Coco's scheme to found a new Catholic community of Indians and creoles, independent and self-sustaining.

His successors rejected that scheme and in the 1970s, the creoles left Platanal. In 1976 the Salesians attempted to create a Plan Pastoral. This Plan Pastoral consisted of four or five-year projects dealing with education; economic cooperatives; catechetical training; a Yanomami language project; teacher training; the development of text books in the Yanomami language and in their cultural context. In large measure, this Pastoral Plan was a response to the criticism of the French anthropologist, Jacques Lizot (1976).

Lizot accused the Salesian missionaries of cultural genocide in their work. He stated that they were attempting to alter the culture of the Yanomami. He particularly attacked their boarding school at L'Esmeralda and the attempt to creolize them at Platanal. Christianization, he argued would render them helpless to defend themselves against the very real threat of outside forces.

The Salesians, instead of fighting Lizot, invited him to collaborate in their work. Lizot began a series of courses in which he instructed the missionaries in basic and applied anthropology. In turn, the Salesians invited him and his archrival, Napoleon Chagnon, to advise them on establishing an intercultural school system at their mission stations. Lizot and Chagnon outlined for the Salesians the challenge they would face in establishing a school that would respect Yanomami culture while preparing them for their role within Venezuela.

Padre Jose Bortoli, an Italian Salesian who also speaks Yanomami and Spanish, states the challenge this way:

> We had to pretend that the Yanomami have an idea of identity as a people and have tools to enter with other people into a Venezuelan identity. We worked for their recognition as Intercultural unit in the Ministry of Education and got that recognition.

The Federal Government presented a Plan for Intercultural Education for all nations within Venezuela and a program for integration in the schools. Interestingly, this plan resulted from the political philosophy of the government in Venezuela, not from the Ministry of Education. The Ministry of Education had perceived indigenous people as waiting for integration into the national culture. The government's plan, however, recognizes the Indians' political and juridical rights in Venezuela and, perhaps, even administrative differences.

The Salesians understood that they had to manage the concept carefully. They are careful to speak of self-help but not *self-determination*. The latter concept raises the specter of possible secession or, at the least, racial conflicts. Self-help, on the other hand, strikes a responsive chord with the bourgeoisie and good conservatives. It evokes an image of cooperative work within the prevailing system as well as a chance to boast about Venezuela's progress regarding "the Indian problem."

With the creation of the government's Intercultural Project, its official recognition of the various peoples and different cultures of Venezuela, the Salesians realized that they were unprepared to do what needed to be done.

> The first thing we did was to meet with anthropological experts in education and economy. It was a very political time, 1976, and on. We consulted with Chagnon, Lizot, Heinon, and other anthropologists. We sent a missionary to study anthropology in Caracas - Ramon Iribertegui. We were open to anthropological ideas . We studied government programs. We investigated a number of issues: the age when kids should be introduced to school; the age when Spanish should be introduced; was it better to go in the morning or afternoon? We studied the concepts of ethnic acculturation, the social processing of language and linguistic problems of biculturalism, the content of the program. We distinguished two forms of context: formal and informal. Much of the content we discovered necessary is too difficult to teach in the school. We decided to let people do what's best done at home. The school, however, supports the home and integrates Yanomami culture within itself. The schools, for example, will reinforce cultural feasts (Bortoli 1994).

Therefore, the schools teach reading, writing, mathematics, and government, among other academic topics. The home, however, teaches the youngsters how to be a Yanomami, their customs, traditions, and beliefs. The Salesians believe that there is no need to teach students how to be a Yanomami but they place Yanomami culture in a high position of respect within the school. They view the Yanomami language as important worthy of respect.

They teach student that what Yanomami do is very important. They are, however, one important people among other important people. The Salesians orient students to a concept of the Yanomami identity being an important identity within a context of other identities. They do not want to put Yanomami culture in a context of crisis. They do not want to create a "victim mentality" among them. It is very important to create an ideology of pride in one's nationhood rather than a desire for conflict in the school. There is no question that there is a problem of teaching a national identity as opposed to a Yanomamo identity. Many non-Indian Brazilians and Venezuelans, for example, are embarrassed by Yanomami and other indigenous peoples, and some even see them as "savages." The problem facing the missionaries is how to get the concept of a broader identity across to them. It is vital for the Yanomami to grasp the concept of their role in the nation-state or they will be eaten alive by it. Even with all the dangers attendant on the rise of ethnicity in the modern world, without a sense of identity there will soon be no Yanomami. Ethnocide, at least in a cultural sense, is always a danger to marginal peoples.

The typical school day begins when the "school bus" picks up those students who do not live near the mission. The "bus" is, of course, not a real bus but a motorized aluminum row boat that plies the river and stops at various settlements to pick up students. Some students, generally those who give more attention and dedication to school, live near mission.

There is also a pre-school with nineteen students at Mavaca. The Salesians sisters teach in this school. They begin teaching children to recognize patterns and symbols from readily present in Yanomami culture. The omnipresent Garfield covered notebooks are used to write and trace these patterns. Once these patterns are mastered. The sisters move on to written language. The little tots write in notebooks and on boards. At this point, they are writing in Yanomami. Additionally, an adapted Spanish system of counting is taught to the Yanomami.

In a joking manner, Bortoli says that the schools are "like stables," the classes in rows next to each other. They are, in fact, well-kept and clean. The ones in the mission stations are made of concrete. There are three post-graduate classes. One was all female. In that class one woman had her own child. Three were obviously pregnant. These post-graduate classes teach more math, geography, culture and the place of the Yanomami in the world. There is a conscious effort to teach "social studies" here, to prepare the

Yanomami for their place in Venezuelan society. They have to speak for themselves to protect their interests and very lives.

Kids are lined up at 8:00 am and a Yanomami headmaster addresses them. No "school bus" is needed at Mavaca. At Mavaca, as elsewhere, the students come with food bowls, and there is some ceremony, some "school tradition." There are about 100 kids at school. There are about 400 Yanomami in immediate area and about 1340 in this section. The school at a nearby small settlement has 33 kids and three teachers trained at Mavaca. Students have decided to have a school uniform consisting of a red loin cloth. Some girls wear a bandanna covering over their breasts.

Because much teaching is done at schools in the shabono, the preparation of Yanomami teachers is continuous. It is a basic tenet of the Salesian Yanomami schools that Yanomami teach other Yanomami. Therefore, teachers are male and female Yanomami with two or three years of education. These teachers go around to the shabonos and hold classes there. The Salesians, themselves trained teachers, check them regularly, every two or three weeks.

As part of the training and supervision, Bortoli joins in teaching of students from time to time. He moves about the room with syllable cards, similar to those Freire used. The students come up and move the cards around the board, forming new sentences, again in the approved Freirean mode. They are shy but eager. The classes are coed.

In one class I observed, IC, there were nine youngsters taking dictation in Yanomami. The pupils had notebooks with Garfield on the front. They first learned syllables in context then moved to dictation. Their teacher went from the chalk board to the youngsters, helping and checking. The overall feeling in the class was pleasant and cooperative.

The nearest shabono is about ten minutes away from the mission station by boat. Others are about seven miles away from the mission station. These teachers go to the Shabonos and begin school about 8:00. There is a break about 10:00 a.m. At 11:30 school is out. The purpose of the break at 10:00 a.m. is two-fold. One is, of course, to let the students get a break from work. The other is to provide food for the Yanomami. The Salesians comprehend the importance of diet. They are keenly aware of various charges leveled at them regarding their spoiling of the Yanomami diet through disturbing their migratory hunting patterns. They are in contact with doctors regarding balanced nutrition. The school meal, served to students and non-students without discrimination, consists of plantains or bananas. In the afternoon, the students have some fish and meat they bring to school along with rice or pasta or manioc or plantains provided by the school. With the notable exception of processed sugar, the Yanomami diet has been significantly improved over the last 30 to 40 years.

Missionaries are also acutely conscious of charges that they are a threat to the culture of the Yanomami.

> Every change, also material change has a cultural significance. Our presence, our missionary presence, is an educational work, and we try to make mediation between other institution like the doctors and the others who came to work here. They look at the Yanomami as if they are cultural problems. They have no idea who the Yanomami are as a people. The Yanomami themselves have no idea who they are as a people among other peoples. They don't know where our intervention leads. They don't have any idea. We don't have any idea. I worry about my work here and wonder if I do any good. I want to keep the Yanomami from being harmed, to help them protect themselves and choose their own destiny.

Therefore, cultural contents from the home are developed in school. For example, although no particular religion is taught in schools, cultural experiences, which take place in school, include religion. These cultural experiences are re-enactments or training for the celebrations that take place in the Shabonos. There are about one per month of these feasts.

A feast I attended, for example, was a "shabono celebration" at the school. The rasha flowers had bloomed the day before signalling the beginning of summer. Fruit is important for these meetings. Some of those important cultural moments are also religious celebrations. In fact, it would be difficult to find one that did not have religious contents. The Salesians note that while these are not Christian celebrations they are life celebrations that are also religious and not in any way in conflict with Christianity. They celebrate food, life, and the rain forest - each and all good and essential to the Yanomami's well-being.

The feast I attended had the children from another village come to the school as their adults would come to the shabono. They landed on the beach and a lookout came, fully decorated in colorful exotic feathers, to announce their arrival. Whoops of joy rang out and the children shivered in expectation. A representative from the visiting group ran into the circle, bursting into song and dance. He thrust his baby spear into the ground in a sign of peace.

The festivities continued in this manner, imitating those of their elders. The feast was about re-enacting and telling the youngsters one of their origin myths. It concerned a father, daughter, and her husband. The daughter saw the palm fruit, a pinion nut. She wanted to climb the tree. Her husband says no. They must go to the forest where there is the true fruit. He gets the fruit but his wife has gone back to her father. There is a hint here of incest. The husband goes mad and cuts his leg. He is transformed into a forest creature. *Pijiqua* is the Yanomami word for rasha. Palm fruit, the pinion nut, is central to the celebration. The youngsters gather in a circle and take turns yelping and imitating forest animal.

Dances, songs, and merriment followed. Banana drinks were consumed and food distributed with great largesse. Gift exchange added more excitement and gaiety to the events. Elders beamed with delight at the actions of their children. One could read their approval of the school in their expressions. No wonder that the first documentary wholly made by the Yanomami is entitled, *The School Is My Home*.

The Salesians are concerned that Yanomami teach other Yanomami. As noted, the teachers are Yanomami. Teachers are paid by the government. There is a problem for Yanomami teachers of being paid at the same scale of other teachers. The Government pays per hour of work because a large number of teachers are needed. As would be expected more than the usual number of teachers are needed in the Yanomami situation. About one teacher per ten students is the typical Yanomami requirement. The Government pays for meals, but not for everything. The Salesian missionaries pay for materials, books, pencils, and transportation even though their Yanomami schools are official schools.

The Salesians train Yanomami teachers in their own land. They are not sent outside to study. Part of the reason for not sending the Yanomami teacher trainees outside to school is simple. There simply there is no indigenous training school for teachers. The government courses for indigenous peoples failed. That, of course, is not the entire explanation. Salesians argue that the Yanomami, by and large, prefer to stay in the forest. For the time being, that is also true. However, the Salesians could, if they desired, provide teacher training outside the forest if they believed that were in Yanomami interests.

I found the Yanomami to be quite curious about the outside world. Indeed, the Salesians admit that there is some curiosity about cities. Travel to Puerto Ayacucho occurs quite frequently. The heads of the Yanomami cooperative travel there on business on a regular basis. Other Yanomami go to hospitals in Puerto Ayacucho for difficult maternity cases, snake bite, or other diseases or medical conditions that cannot be easily treated in the forest. Some Yanomami take advantage of their privilege to free flights to go to Caracas to visit. Moreover, Yanomami representatives have presented their people's case to government officials in the capital. Certainly, it seems hard to imagine that within ten years many more will not be in Venezuela's big cities.

The educational content further stimulates Yanomami curiosity about the world outside the forest. The course contents were taken from Ministry of Education's Common Program and its Special Program for Indian Culture. The Salesians adapted these programs to the Yanomami situation. There was a need for adaptation because Indian culture is not homogeneous. Some of the other Amazonian Indian peoples have virtually lost their indigenous culture. Fortunately, that is not the case with the Yanomami.

An important part of the curriculum adaptation concerned preparation of text books that reflected Yanomami culture and its concerns. This preparation was undertaken because of the importance of having the Yanomami see themselves as significant people among other significant peoples. Their language and culture are vital, and they must come to accept that importance in face of insults hurled at them by miners and others who lust after their land. The Yanomami now know that there are many people in the world but they must come to understand that they are equal with the others.

Therefore, all the contents of their text books and all that is taught in the school is about their culture and the interrelation with the other culture. The purpose is to know that they are as important as other peoples. They have no reason to be ashamed of themselves when they go outside. The school's attempt to convey to them that they should say with pride "I am Yanomami." The school seeks to present this message in an integrated manner coordinating many activities, not only writing and reading, but also playing and cultural activities. The Salesian decision to have the schools not only near the mission for the people who live near, but also in the shabonos must be seen in that light. Those shabono schools can teach the children when it is most convenient to them, adapting class time to the seasons of the year and the activities of those seasons. They are incorporated into the same intercultural system.

There was a problem with the transcription of the Yanomami language. Because everybody, every anthropologist and every had "his own story and his own system." The Salesians tried to unify the system. They asked the ministry of education to define the transcription system. That was a useful political decision because in the future they cannot easily change that. It is very important that every literate Yanomami will know the language in the same system because doing so will strengthen their underlying unity.

In school, as has been stated previously, Yanomami learn things that they are not taught in their homes. The philosophy of the intercultural school is that the best school is in their homes. Therefore, the Salesians insist that pupils have to stay at home when there is an activity there. They are not to come to school on those days. Indeed, the school participates also in the activity of their shabono. The shabono invites the school to all the feasts. Conversely, the school invites the adults to what happens here.

The philosophy of the intercultural school sees no conflict between home and school. Students have to participate in the activities of their home. Because language is a vital part of personal and ethnic identity, they must realize that their language is very important. Therefore, the text books are in Yanomami in the early years and then in Yanomami and Spanish. The purpose is to give them a book as other people have but one in which their language and their spiritual perspective are treated as important. Simply put, they see themselves in the book rather than Spaniards or Venezuelans. There are six books that are in Yanomami or on Yanomami topics. These books help them to see themselves portrayed as they wish, not as the object of outsiders.

The teaching of Spanish is part of the intercultural philosophy. It begins in the 1D class. It gives the Yanomami an instrument to help them deal with outsiders. It is a valuable tool in the inevitable contact with others. To ease that contact, then, the intercultural school teaches that the Yanomami can remain Yanomami while being also Venezuelans.

Toward that same end teachers place kids' pictures of Yanomami scenes on the walls. Simon Bolivar was also on the wall, an attempt to underscore the national identity. The shabono and the liberator belong to the Yanomami, both are part of Venezuela.

Part of this preparation for democratic defense within the Venezuelan context takes place in the "post-graduate" school. Many boys and girls want to finish something and feel that the primary school is just the beginning and not the end of education. A number of Yanomami asked for more education. They wanted cultural education, geography, mathematics, citizenship training, and other courses in that vein. Therefore, missionaries initiated the post-graduate class and offer it twice a week in the afternoon. People come back to school and go on with their learning. They do not yet want to leave the forest to continue school. The post-graduate class develops more social subjects. The Yanomami are introduced to more complex aspects of living in Venezuela. Problems in regard to land and garampeiros get discussed. The importance of cooperatives, trade with foreigners, critical problems of cultural change, and the future of the Yanomami are addressed. Most of the students who attend this class are engaged in some political or social work. They are teachers and leaders in some way. Importantly, these people include women. It is in this school that missionaries teach.

These schools were begun in 1976 and consequently they have had a good deal of time to develop. Although the typical graduate is too old to go on to higher education right now, there is little doubt that in the near future Yanomami will be found in schools in Puerto Ayacucho and other Venezuelan cities. Currently, people are completing the primary schools at a younger age and soon it would be possible to send them on to higher studies. The Salesians think it would be difficult for Yanomami to adapt to other system of studies. They argue that they would need at least one more year to learn a more colloquial Spanish. But even as they present these arguments, it is clear that they realize that within ten years, substantial numbers of Yanomami will be educated, at least partially, in schools outside the Amazon rain forest.

Since 1976 Salesian schools have trained approximately 350 students per year including the extensions. Ocamo has trained about 80 students per year and Mavaca about 100. Men have a greater opportunity of attending school. Girls depend on their husband to continue school since they get married young and have children soon after. However, a good number of people finish 6th grade. In general women attend until they are 11 or 12 and men until they are 16. However, I saw evidence that many married women with children were currently attending school and had no embarrassment about attending even the lower grades with small children. I also saw married women attending the post-graduate school. In some classes, there were as many women as men. The implications of this development for the future development of Yanomami culture and male-female relations requires some thought.

One criticism of the Salesians' educational project has come from Napoleon Chagnon (Chagnon in press). Chagnon criticizes the Salesians for not adequately preparing the Yanomami for protecting their own needs. Moreover, he claims that they are so changing the Yanomami that they may destroy their culture. The Salesians have to defend themselves on two fronts. They have to point to their attempts to incorporate the Yanomami in their own self-development and, concurrently, demonstrate that such incorporation does not destroy the Yanomami culture.

On the first front, they point out that literate Yanomami are trained in health services and in teaching.

The missionaries state that their final goal is to train the Yanomami as doctors, nurses, and other health professionals but it is hard for Yanomami to go away to study. On the other hand, Yanomami have no compunction about cooperating in their medical treatment. They come and they tell missionaries what the problems are, and they recommend how medicine should be introduced into their own areas. For instance, they would rather be with the family and the same medicine would be more important if given by a friend than by a stranger. So they will eagerly explain their medical concepts to anyone who will listen to them. It is this willingness to participate in their changes with sympathetic outsiders that encourages the Salesians in promoting the intercultural concept.

Almost all the Yanomami teachers are Yanomami, except for those in the post-graduate and nursery schools. The Salesians have plans for transference of these currently non-paid posts when there are Yanomami who have adequate experience of the outside world to train their fellows.

The Salesians desire to effect appropriate change with as little disruption as possible to the Yanomami sociocultural system. To that end they have worked to have the cooperatives, schools, and doctors go to the shabonos so that the Yanomami do not have to come to center.

I asked the Yanomami whether the missionaries prevent them from being Yanomami. They answered "No." They themselves want to dre___ ___ keep away mosquitos. The missionaries do not make them ___ forest they put off their clothe___ ___, so why can't they? Should they ___ ___? They said, repeatedly in what ___ a Yanomami, I see like a Yano___ ___ Yanomami. Therefore, I am a Ya___ ___othes, do not keep me from bein___ ___at makes me a Yanomami."

F___ ___ their life and presence to do their preaching ___ ___al sermons. Many Yanomami ask why the Salesians are in the Amazon. They note that the mission presence is different from that of others. Ask about the missionaries' feelings and their praying in chapel. The Salesians judge that their role is to teach:

> 1) that our God is not against them -they are not less important - our God is also their God; 2) with their contact more of their beliefs must become problematic - scientific ideas makes their world view problematic. It is important to give an alternative faith that supports their change. In school, for example, scientific view challenges their mythic vision. We try to emphasize that the scientific and religious are two separate visions not opposing ones. We also say that there are many ways to go to the same "shabono." Every street is important, autonomous. Each needs respect. For example, their vision of stars and the moon are very mythological. We explain that a sacred vision is different. Every vision has a particular function or purpose. There are distinct visions but are both important.

The Salesians wisely understand that Western education itself challenges basic traditional religious beliefs. It is essential to remember that the Salesian Order is primarily a teaching order. Bortoli and the other Salesians, including Bishop Velasco, understand the manner in which intellectual Christianity has struggled with the relationship between scientific and sacred views of the world. Therefore, when Bortoli states that "the purpose of the Christian faith is a service we can offer to explain the new vision," he is not repeating clichés. He is speaking from a profound theological conviction, that of liberation and inculturationist theology. He makes that clear when he indicates the manner in which the Salesians incorporate the customary system in their vision of Christianity to help teach Yanomami people that they are an important people. They tell them that God sends "first men" to give religion to each people and teach religion to them. All religion and all culture, they affirm, comes from God. Any imperfections in these sacred systems come from human error.

To understand the Salesian educational strategy it is necessary to understand it within the entire context of their Freirean derived theory of change in which the people undergoing change must take charge of their own destiny.

Thus, Padre Bortoli states, "The most important things for the Yanomami are goods - if we bring these to them they don't have to come to the center."

Bortoli responds to Chagnon's criticism of the Salesians as running a theocratic state, that the Salesians are not a theocracy. The President of each member shabono helps plan the cooperative's work. There are two representatives of the cooperative, SUYAO, in Puerto Ayacucho. The cooperatives were started with a self-help philosophy. In 1957 the missionaries gave goods for nothing, prompting older Yanomami to say that "The first missionaries were better!"

SUYAO's organization is developing into a representative unit of Yanomami for work and trading processes. It was established in 1986. Its farm works have been approved by the appropriate agricultural branch of the Venezuelan government. As originally constituted, it had an elected President, Vice President, and Secretary. There was a General Assembly and Council of Elders.

Its Objectives are rather straight forward to: try to make Yanomami life better; trade goods; participate in politics; hold meetings to discuss problems and projects; and defend Yanomami culture. There has been one major change in SUYAO's central constitution in light of these objectives. Economic questions were being settled by the central organization. The family, however, is the central mechanism of Yanomami society. Therefore, preservation and strengthening of the family was a major concern.

The Yanomami changed the constitution. There are currently four District Presidents and each has a secretariat and council and elders. Each works for trade and politics. For example, they are concerned with foreigners coming into the area. They try to make peace between shabonos, and trade with distant communities where needed.

SUYAO has, also, undertaken a number of projects: honey; shirts; and farina production. It is impossible to send farm products to market but they can send farina and other processed food to market. The Salesians looked for projects that would not cause great change in Yanomami system of work nor harm the forest ecology. Thus, among their projects have been the cultivation and processing of honey and plantains. "People only need to cultivate, put in sun then mash. And it's also good food for children (Bortoli 1994)."

SUYAO's interchange of needed goods is going well. It is not self-sufficient yet but people participate more and more actively. Bortoli is concerned that warfare still continues in the area but has hopes that as the Yanomami begin to cultivate greater interdependence and understand their need for solidarity, they will begin to decrease their internal conflicts.

To understand the overall purpose of SUYAO, it is necessary to realize that there is no single Yanomami council. There is no single traditional Yanomami leader. SUYAO was created so that the Yanomami would have a representative body which outsiders could understand. The Salesians realize that there is no traditional Yanomami representative system. There is no Yanomami council or chief. The Yanomami are very independent. Every family in the shabono is and independent political entity. Each family has its own head. Old people have moral, but not political, power. The Yanomami meet among themselves and speak openly in meetings. The meetings will arrive at a decision but everybody is free to do as he wishes.

Bortoli agrees with Chagnon that one has to be careful of self-proclaimed representatives of the Yanomami who are not really very representative people. In general, these representatives are young people who speak Spanish to a certain extent. They are also able to contact Venezuelans or Brazilians, but, according to Bortoli, they are not representative of their people. To be representative, he states, you have to meet with everybody and to speak with them. That is an impossible task in the Amazon.

Like Chagnon, Bortoli is afraid that some of the young spokespeople might be manipulated by outside interests. Although they disagree on particular leaders, Bortoli, for example, has high regard for Davi Kopinawa of Brazil, they do agree on the dangers unscrupulous outsiders pose to naive young men. Therefore, a bit of paternalism creeps into their talk similar to that I have noted elsewhere (Salamone 1994).

The Salesians believe that in certain cases, for the time being, they have to be speaking for the Yanomami. They have to champion their interests. Some problems require immediate response, for instance the problem of the creation of the Yanomami National Park. The Salesians had to represent Yanomami interests because there was no time for asking everybody's opinion. Moreover, according to the Salesians, the Yanomami do not care whether this forest is Yanomami or not. For the rain forest people there is not the same problem, as for the Andean people. For the Yanomami the land is not their mother or grandmother. They do not have that type of mystical relationship with the land as so many other Indian peoples do. Therefore, it does not matter to the Yanomami, in this interpretation, which land they have. Any land that will produce food is good. Bortoli is concerned, therefore, that the Yanomami will not move to protect the rain forest if they get a better offer. This contradiction in trusting the people is a significant one and will be discussed in the last chapter.

Bortoli is also sensitive to anthropological criticisms he has received over the years. Therefore, he was quick to note in interviews with me that the groups who live near the mission station

... were here at the beginning; they didn't come here because the mission was here. There is just one group here who fled from a war at Platanal. They say they feel safer here. They abandoned their shabono and moved to the other side. They came here for protection from war. There were no doctors at their shabono for two years. They were abandoned. Some innovations have taken place and now there is a doctor. They live in Ocamo because it is furthest away from their enemies and war. Each place before Ocamo they had gone to there was a war.

It is important to note that no Yanomami groups come to the missions to stay in school. If a Yanomami lives too far to attend school, their family may come to live with relatives who are nearby and then attend school. There is no boarding school for Yanomami. This policy appears to be a reaction to Lizot's mid-1970s criticism of the L'Esmeralda boarding school for Yanomami. Lizot, as I have noted, has had a great deal of input in planning the teaching content and materials along with the Salesians.

The connection of the Salesians' work with that of Friere and other liberation theologians becomes quite clear when the following material is considered. The Salesians argue that human culture is a gift of God for self-development and for a people's attainment of humanity. They contrast this position with that which they perceive to be the fundamentalist's view. The Salesians thus argue that culture is fundamentally good. They do not maintain that everything is good but they argue that they Yanomami themselves know that not everything in their culture is good. The Yanomami, they say, do not want the bad in their culture.

> All of us know what is evil. They know it is not good to kill. They know murder is wrong. Every people tries to avoid the bad consequences of their culture. There are many differences because of human egoism. We are fundamentally positive in our view of culture. In dialogues we say that the Yanomami style is fundamentally positive. It is as important as others. It is a good culture and they are not outsiders to God.

Bortoli admits that his is an inculturationist and incarnationist theology in which it is very important to transmit the message - not a literal translation but symbolic translation, one that goes to meaningful translation. It is important to him to translate Christ's incarnation into terms of the people's culture. He holds that the Gospel must also be inculturated into people's culture.

We missionaries cannot be insensitive, neither can we change our own culture. But Yanomami accept and appreciate us. The anthropologists who play at being Yanomami are ridiculous. But we must know who we are and who Yanomami are. There is a clear interest in identity. Dialogue is better, for we must respect each other.

Salvation, for the Salesians, is an intercultural operation. They say that they do not want the creoles to become Yanomami or vice-versa. Many things may interpenetrate, they assert, but they do not see that as assimilation. They argue that we have to see interculturalism in the political process. It is not a scholarly problem. It must manifest itself in the political context - both Venezuelan and international. Its test comes in living in the rain forest, in frontier conflict, the possibility of tourism, and in many other ways. It must be seen in an international context. It must be, from Bortoli's perspective, a contact between equals.

Perhaps, to anthropologists it should be theoretical but it is not. Reality is different. What happens is not so clear or academic. The mission has to be a mediator/broker. It has to be a mediator in political context and that is not so easy. We cannot ever predict what happens. We have chosen to put options to the Yanomami. We have to hear the Indians and prefer their choices. Not because they are poor but because of their values. The question is always the same, no? Is it useful or do the Yanomami really need school and so on. But the answer depend from what do you think of the future of these people. Do you think that they may remain isolated, is it possible? But while they're alone, to know their own culture is important. Well, what is important of their culture to maintain? There are some things that change. They want to change. They want - they look at something, and they want to just to have it.

The missionaries have to combat the old romantic primitivism of some anthropologists as well as others who view the Yanomami as if it were possible for people to stay in a Garden of Eden forever. Most anthropologists realize that this remaining in a fictional Garden of Eden never happens. People are always changing. For the missionaries, then, the real problem involves hegemonic issues. Certainly, the Yanomami are an endangered people. They face the power of other cultures who desire their land and the resources on that land. The missionaries provide a continuing presence. They can translate the world to the Yanomami and the Yanomami to the world. As Bortoli notes, it is not an easy nor enviable task.

Chapter 9

Chagnon's Response to His Critics

Frank A. Salamone, based on the transcripts of Chagnon's speech on November 2, 1994, at the American Anthropological Association at Frank A. Salamone's Session on "Anthropology and Theology"

Chagnon acknowledges that his dispute with the Salesians has been one of the ugliest debates in the entire history of anthropology. He believes that the manner in which the debate began is a mystery to both anthropologists and missionaries in general. Chagnon stated his desire to effect a reconciliation between himself and those anthropologists who have defended him and missionaries in general, and the Salesians in particular. He desires to behind this extraordinarily ugly discussion. This discussion has been featured in the various media.

He is concerned that it is taking attention away form the Yanomami themselves, who should be the focus of concern. After all, differences between missionaries and anthropologists should be subsidiary to the plight of the Yanomami. Certainly, both the Salesians and anthropologists are very much concerned with advancing their chances for a better future for them.

Chagnon states that he desires to work with the Salesians and Dr. Teodoro Marcano on a health project. That project is important both for the Yanomami and for those for whom they have become a symbol; namely, all tribesmen. For that reason, it is important that people work together to advance the cause of the Yanomami. If they do not survive, then other tribal peoples who are less known and less recognizable to the world at large will also fail to survive.

Along with others who are concerned for the Yanomami, Chagnon believes that the Yanomami should speak for themselves. However, he also agrees with others similarly concerned that right now, the question of who should speak for the Yanomami is an extraordinarily complex question, the answer to which no one currently has. It will be a very long time before the Yanomami can in fact democratically speak for themselves.

There are, according to Chagnon, some false impressions being given in the press. The press implies that there is a unified Yanomami nation that speaks with one voice. Moreover, it fosters the image that the Brazilian Yanomami are different from those in Venezuela. Perhaps, it is because they have heard more about the Brazilian situation. In particular, the rise of Davi Kopinawa, a Brazilian Yanomami, has focussed attention on the Brazilian situation. Gradually, people in the West have assumed that Davi is chief of all Yanomami, not simply a representative of one small group of Yanomami.

Chagnon is concerned about this situation. While he believes Davi Kopinawa to be an honorable spokesman for his people, he suspects that a non-Yanomami is scripting his material. Moreover, the miners have paraded a Yanomami leader who purports to represent all Venezuelan Yanomami and who wants to give away all their gold. The danger of manipulating Yanomami even for good causes is that someone else will appear to manipulate them for bad ones.

The real situation is that Venezuela is full of Yanomami villages in the Orinoco- Mavaquita area. Not all of them have been in similar contact with the outside world. Chagnon noted that a few villages have been in direct contact with Salesian missions in Venezuela for at least thirty to forty years and are well on the way to acculturization, are becoming very sophisticated in knowledge and awareness of the external world and are in fact the particular villages from which the leaders of the Yanomami are being recruited. He noted that other groups of Yanomami are associated with other missions such as the New Tribes missions. In common with the Salesians these missionaries have people whom they are

putting forward as spokesmen for at least their villages.
Chagnon then got to the nub of his argument:

> But right now in terms of the question that Frank Salamone put as
> the title of this topic, "Who Speaks for the Yanomami?", it is
> becoming at this point more and more a situation in which a
> handful of Yanomami at Salesian villages, individuals who are very
> bright to have competence in Spanish, are actually speaking to the
> Salesians who then speak to selected people from the outside world
> such as anthropologists who don't know the Yanomami or the
> press or politicians or agencies who then communicate what this
> information is to an outside world that is indeed much more
> complex than the unified whole outside world, and I've tried to
> indicate that ... But in fact what the needs and interests are of
> those Yanomami who now have been in contact at these particular
> mission posts for 35-40 years are not necessarily identical to or
> consistent with the needs of the Yanomami who are more isolated,
> more into the interior.

Chagnon stated that the answer to the question of "Who Speaks
for the Yanomami?" is that particular Yanomami need to speak to
the particular issues of specific groups of Yanomami and their
needs. There are, of course, some fundamental, basically universal,
needs that cross-cut all Yanomami settlements. But at the moment
we are at a point in the development of Yanomami self-awareness
where a handful of individuals, a handful of ideas, can make an
enormous difference in the future of the Yanomami, determine
their political awareness, and their entire general stance as they
become more and more incorporated into national and international
areas of economics and politics. Chagnon warned that we have to
give very serious consideration to the question of what kinds of
information should the Yanomami have? That question raises further ones concerns who should provide needed information to the
Yanomami. Moreover, how can we provide the Yanomami with a
sense of democracy without imposing our own ideas concerning
their path of development on them? These are serious questions, for
we do not simply want them to parrot back our own ideas to us.
   Certainly, it is at Salesian villages and other points of contact
where the Yanomami are going to gradually acquire the kind of
sophistication   and   political   awareness   and   a   sense   of
Yanomami-ness that is going to be fundamental for them to deal

ultimately with the complex issues that they are going to face as they become articulated more intimately with an external world. Chagnon warns that this process will not happen overnight. There is a need, therefore, for those more acculturated mission Yanomami to represent fairly more remote Yanomami, such as those who live in the Chiapas area.

Chagnon listed a number of major concerns that will face the Yanomami. Health is first on the list. As he noted, "And with the gold rush that began in 1987, problems of health that already existed among the Yanomami were severely complicated by the introduction of new diseases or making epidemic diseases like malaria that were already there to begin with. And I think this is probably for the Yanomami the central single most important and urgent issue for us to concern ourselves about." Sanitary problems in the villages have been in contact with outsiders for thirty years or forty years are a major problem. These village people are relatively sedentary.

Chagnon called attention to the problem of land. Pressure must be kept on the governments of Brazil and Venezuela even though for the time being they have promulgated laws that have virtually guaranteed the Yanomami access to and exclusive rights to their land. However, in Brazil the military and the government keeps nibbling away at concessions that they have already made. There is, furthermore, a history in Brazil has of reneging on guarantees. Currently, there is a new geo-political designation called the Biosphere Reserve for which in Venezuela there are no political antecedents or precedents. A whole new set of rules is going to have to be determined. Chagnon is concerned that people pay very close attention to the situation "because what rules are set up in this Biosphere Reserve is going to determine who can go in it and what kinds of use can be made of it." He is delighted that Padre Jose Bortoli is involved in the process, for he trusts Bortoli and hopes that Bortoli will stay in touch with him regarding the situation. He suggests that perhaps the Salesian missionaries could keep Americans informed about the situation of the Yanomami in Venezuela so that all our Yanomami information is not about the Brazilian Yanomami. Chagnon is also concerned that the Yanomami have a voice in how their land is developed in the new biosphere areas.

In a change from his more traditional position, Chagnon is concerned with the possibility of protein deficiency in those sedentarized areas in which the Yanomami have been living for thirty or forty years. He notes that something has to be done "to supplement or provide to the Yanomami ways of supplementing their nutritional needs, particularly in the form of protein and I hope that you don't tell Marvin Harris that I said that."

Education and training form another area of concern. Chagnon asks how many Yanomami should be educated and what sort of education should they have. There is no question that the Yanomami are going to have to learn about the external world. However, Chagnon calls for a more democratic educational system.

> They're getting certain sets of ideas and not other sets of ideas. And if I had one fundamental complaint with, not only Salesians, but the new tribes missions, is that they should democratize and make more open the kinds of ideas that are presented to them in these schools that the Salesians and the other mission groups are operating.

The area of human and political rights is a vital one. For at least the time being, Chagnon states, non-Yanomami will have to safeguard these rights. Until the Yanomami acquire their political self-awareness to the point where they can in a sophisticated and effective way fight for themselves, others will have to do a lot of fighting for them. Chagnon thinks that the number of Yanomami in Brazil and Venezuela allowed into Western Civilization should be limited until what our society has to offer to people like the Yanomami improves. We need to offer opportunities that are desirable and dignified.

> I think it's just insane to cause them to become westernized to give them a taste of the things that they would like to have but could never acquire. And until we can provide opportunities in Brazil and Venezuela for them to enter into the national light in a manner that's dignified and admirable, the rate at which we force them to be enculturated should be given very considerable thought because, in fact, we're asking them to give up something of value that is going to cost them a great deal in order to acquire something that may be of much less value.

There are a variety of viewpoints among the Yanomami. There is a need for Yanomami to become more cooperative and collaborative. They are not now a democratic people. Chagnon points out that their form of government has very little to do with the kinds of things that Americans assume other peoples are all about. He warns that we must be cautious when a leader steps forward and says he speaks for all the Yanomami that any deals we make with that leader "do not necessarily reflect what all other Yanomami are interested in." The situation is similar to what happened over and over again in the history of the United States where one chief would make an agreement but another chief would refuse to accept it. Soon the United States would attack the entire tribe because one portion broke its word.

Chagnon believes that much of what will happen in the future will require some kind of permanent predictable cash income. He argues that there are two ways of resolving that inevitable problem. One is developing "ways for the Yanomami themselves to acquire self-sufficiency and produce something that has economic value on a local or regional or even a national or international market." It demands considerable thought be given to what kinds of things they should be encouraged to produce. He notes that Bortoli and the Salesians have worked to get the Yanomami involved in this endeavor. They have started projects in the production of honey, cocoa, and coffee - things that will not interfere dramatically with their own subsistence patterns. In turn they may produce something useful for the world market. Chagnon states that:

> The other obvious way to look at this is to provide some sorts of subsidies for them, either from the Venezuelan government itself or from international agencies, or from NGOs. But all of these things that are going to be required for the Yanomami to speak for themselves, as Frank Salamone put it, and become articulated to a western culture, are going to eventually cost money. And it's got to come from somewhere.

Chapter 10

Conclusion

Frank A. Salamone

The Yanomami have become a symbol of all marginal and endangered peoples. Napoleon Chagnon brought the Yanomami to the attention of the world over 25 years ago and has maintained an abiding interest in their survival. The Salesian missionaries have also had an enduring and long history of caring for the Yanomami. Indeed, Padre Coco began the mission at Ocamo about forty years ago. Appropriately, Chagnon and the Salesians have collaborated amicably on many occasions. In fact, he has worked with the New Tribes Mission and Dr. Marcano as well.

These ties serve to illustrate the intimate nature of the Upper Orinoco world. Certainly, I could demonstrate other links among all who work among the Yanomami in Brazil as well as Venezuela. The family-like nature of the community of workers goes a great distance in explaining the intensity of feelings that flared up, not for the first time, in the Salesian-Chagnon dispute. Earlier battles had been fought between Jaques Lizot and the Salesians, anthropologists and the New Tribes missions and Catholic and Protestant mission groups.

These battles concerning who has the best approach to helping the Yanomami, however, often divert people's attention from concentrating their efforts on aiding the Yanomami. Fortunately, each participant in this book acknowledges that fact. Each contributor seeks to find a means for encouraging collaborative efforts with others who complement his efforts. At the same time, each seeks to listen more effectively to the Yanomami themselves.

Of course, the Yanomami do not speak with a single voice. In that sense, no *one* speaks for the Yanomami. Nevertheless, there *are* certain evident themes underlying the messages of the many voices found within any society, even those societies that value independence and individuality. The greater the Yanomami contact with those whom they deem "outsiders," for example, the more they understand the need for protecting the land. At one time, they could afford to take the land for granted. There was so much of it and so few of them. They now realize that those times of lack of worry regarding land ownership have passed. They are now wiser in seeing through the bribes of those who wish to soften them up for exploitation through feigned friendliness.

Moreover, there is now a great value placed on practical education among the Yanomami, for women as well as men. Those Yanomami who live near the mission stations want their own medical workers, teachers, traders, shop keepers, and representatives. They are clear in wanting their own spokespeople in the centers of power, and to that end they want to learn Spanish. Venezuela has gone to a multicultural-multilingual educational system and a number of Yanomami are taking advantage of these schools. Interestingly and significantly, all Yanomami schools are totally under missionary control.

Yanomami have place a high cultural value on caring for one's self. Thus, they frequently mention the value of learning modern farming methods, using good farm implements, trading, and adapting modern ways to the Yanomami way of life. The also place a high value on speaking Spanish in order to "speak for ourselves in the government." This awareness of representative processes in interesting in the light of debates on how ready the Yanomami are to represent themselves. Both missionaries and anthropologists have sometimes seemed afraid at times to "trust" the Yanomami with making their own decisions, a rather understandable if paternalistic position. Perhaps, the question is how ready are those who have been interpreting for the Yanomami to let the Yanomami speak for themselves?

It must be granted that Yanomami who have had little contact with outsiders do not display the wariness of them that marks those who have. They appear eager to get into contact with those who can supply them with modern trade goods. They even suspect other Yanomami of inventing horror stories to keep them from getting into contact with outsiders. Certainly, these more isolated Yanomami have not yet had the disillusioning experiences with outsiders that those in contact have had. They have not had the misfortune of having been cheated by miners or seen women raped and stolen by outsiders who deem Indians as less than humans.

Yanomami, in spite of their reputation as "the fierce people," appear tired of warfare. As Cesar Diminawa stated, "I have killed but I am not a killer!" I found it difficult to believe that the Yanomami's repeated statements in favor of peace and a safe life were merely rhetorical flourishes. Reiterations of a desire for a long, peaceful, healthy life for themselves and their children in which they did not have to worry about sudden death, struck me as authentic cries from the heart. Many Yanomami have sought to relocate themselves at or near mission stations where the dangers of sudden attacks and ambushes are lessened.

Certainly, Chagnon raises a valid issue in wondering whether this sedentarization of a hitherto nomadic people poses a threat to the microenvironment and to their own health and overall well-well-being. Simply put, will this sedentarization lead to over-hunting? Will it change their dietary habits? Will any of these possible changes pose health risks for the Yanomami? If so, what are these risks and how can they be handled? How can needed changes be introduced with minimum damage to the people, their society, and culture? Who are the best people to handle this introduction?

The Salesians and New Tribes missionaries display an acute awareness of these problems. They are not complacent in dealing with them. Neither are they shying away from their implications. They offer various solutions, including further collaborative research with anthropologists and medical personnel, including epidemiologists. The biosphere and national park approach have proven useful elsewhere under United Nations and national auspices and have been launched in Venezuela and Brazil. They, too, have helped bring international attention to the plight of the Yanomami. Their astute analyses and scientific approaches to medicine and public health have belied the stereotypes that often bedevil their work.

They insist that they are not there to force conversions nor to neglect the material needs of the people.

Dr. Teo Marcano presents a valuable medical insight into Yanomami health problems. Lack of adequate funds, negative stereotypes, political realities and difficult living conditions for medical personnel all contribute to the challenge of delivering essential health services to the Yanomami. Many Venezuelans are ashamed of the "primitiveness" of the Yanomami and other Amazonian peoples. They see little point in expending scarce resources on people whom they deem unproductive. Certainly, training indigenous health care personnel is a vital requirement in moving toward solving health care delivery problems for the Yanomami.

Marcano, moreover, strongly illustrates the basic significance of anthropological knowledge and techniques in the development process. He indicates that a medical doctor is relatively helpless in delivering health care to the Yanomami without a detailed familiarity and understanding of their own medical cognitive maps. Until he himself learned to see the medical world from a Yanomami perspective, he could not begin to teach them about western medicine. He had no language into which to translate these concepts. Until he felt reasonably familiar with their medical culture and language, he did not even attempt to instruct them about western medical concepts and practices.

He knew it would be useless to try. Once he understood their medical "language," Marcano could begin to translate western concepts for the Yanomami. To aid him he enlisted the aid of local practitioners. This assistance enabled him to make some headway in his efforts but it also led him to note the tie between religion and medicine. Therefore, Marcano had to gain some insight into the Yanomami religious cosmology, for the medical and religious systems are intricately tied together. Without a knowledge of religious practices and ideas, Marcano faced a dead-end in his work.

This insight provides a lesson for all who seek to launch development projects, including anthropologists. Religion, medicine, anthropology, and the people's own desires are integral parts of any effort to aid the Yanomami. Clashes, therefore, among representatives of these groups are counterproductive. Not only do they prevent the missionary, anthropologist, and health practitioner from serving the people's needs, the only justifiable reason for their being in Yanomami territory, they also draw international attention away from the main show of the dangers to the marginalized and endangered peoples to the side show of petty squabbling.

This book has attempted to promote cooperation and understanding so that the cause of the Yanomami may be furthered. It is the hope of each participant that the day may come soon that they Yanomami may speak for themselves and not require any interpreters to make their wishes known to "outsiders." Truly, they seem ready to assume that position soon and while they may not speak with one voice, it would be foolish to expect or desire any democratic and independent people to do so.

Student Questions

1. On what sort of issues do the Yanomami seem to have reached some type of agreement? Why?

2. What factors may account for differences in Yanomami opinion?

3. Why is cooperation among development agents so vital to Yanomami interests?

4. In what ways do medicine, anthropology, and missionary work complement one another?

5. What factors led to a dispute between Chagnon and the Salesians? What might be done to avoid this type of dispute in the future?

6. In your opinion what are the major issues facing the Yanomami and how might they be solved?

ENDNOTES

1. This amicable discussion occurred at the 1994 Annual Meetings of the American Anthropological Association in Atlanta, Georgia, at the session I chaired entitled Anthropology and Theology. Further discussion ensued at Luisa Margolies's workshop on indigenous peoples in Venezuela.

2. For newspaper treatment of the issues see sources in the references cited section.

3. The situation, in brief, is that a Yanomami group came to the area to re-establish an alliance. Two Yanomami villages were established near Protestant missions and the third upstream. A fourth was a previous enemy whose people wanted to stabilize an uneasy peace . The third village provoked the war that Chagnon describes. In sum, the behavior that Chagnon describes did occur but it was behavior exhibited during a period of extreme pressure under threat of war and during a ruinous epidemic.

4. The Salesians wrote a bitter response to Brewer Carias in 1991, *Consideraciones a un Documento de Charles Brewer Carias*. They signed as "Un Grupo de Missionaros del Alto Orinoco". Basically, the Salesians objected to the unbalanced nature of Brewer Carias's development plans. The very thing which Chagnon who allied himself with Brewer Carias later accused the Salesians of planing! Chagnon has since broken with Brewer Carias and admits he was taken in by his ideas. Luisa Margolies (April 3,1995) wrote "I feel that Chagnon's motivation is far more complex than summed up. He really did not concoct the biosphere scheme. Biosphere movements had been going on for years, generated by the IVIC ecology department (going back 20 years, I believe). Chagnon's friendship (genuine) with Brewer Carias is long-standing. Brewer Carias himself had worked on a type of biosphere project in La Neblina, partially funded by the American Museum of Natural History. Brewer Carias has mining interests in the Amazon, a fact denied by Chagnon, and this has created an enormous conflict of interest.

5. These conclusion are based on a phone conversation with Terence Turner on November 2, 1994. Turner later repeated the salient points at the American Anthropological Association meetings on December 2 in my session on Anthropology and Theology and in other sessions, most notably that on Missionaries and Human Rights.

6. Such a position reverses Chagnon's earlier one regarding the sociobiological sources of warfare and places him in Marvin Harris's camp, a reversal Chagnon acknowledged at the 1994 American Anthropological Association session on Anthropology and Theology. (See Harris 1984 and

Good 1987 and 1989 for the outlines of the debate.)

7. Transcript of Anthropology and Theology Session December 2, 1994.

8. I investigated Chagnon's charges thoroughly. I found that the Salesians had never sold rifles to the Yanomami. The Yanomami cooperative SUYAO had sold rifles which they had obtained from the missionaries, the total was either five or six depending on the person relating the tale. All agreed that the Salesians put a stop to the practice, anticipating that the rifles might be used for warfare. In any event, there are hundreds of rifles in Yanomami hands. Most come from Brazil but some come from the Venezuelan National Guard who sell old rifles to the Yanomami. It is not against the law for any Venezuelan citizen, including Yanomami, to have rifles in the bush. Some Yanomami state that Chagnon himself sold a rifle to a Yanomami.

9. Lizot (1994) *American Anthropologist*.

10. Asch 1991. Asch and Chagnon broke with each other after years of collaborating.

11. Finkers . Finkers is a remarkable naturalist and ethnographer. The Yanomami bring him specimens of any unusual plant or animal they come across. His notebooks are examples of punctilious recorded and drawn observations. There is little about the Yanomami or their environment that he does not know. He speaks the language fluently and has an easy relationship with them.

12. Donald Delaney, a Salesian, who accompanied me to Venezuela, was adamant on that point. He pointed out just how powerful the Salesians were in many countries, including Venezuela, where their educational work meant that they had trained many of the leaders of various countries.

13. It was with some effort that Delaney and I persuaded Cappelletti to remain cool and not hire a psychologist to do a profile on Chagnon, for example. Cappelletti ranted that he would spend $20000 on such a study. He also entertained thoughts of mounting an anthropological expedition to discredit Chagnon's anthropological work. While such displays of temper must be taken with a grain of salt, they do hint at serious contemplation with further action, including lawsuits.

14. Cardozo E-mailed me "... although I am very much interested in sociobiology (evolutionary psychology as it is now called), I don't agree with all its tenets. Also, although Chagnon was the head of my doctoral committee, I never took classes from him. I had finished course work when Chagnon was hired at UCSB and he never taught graduate seminars at that

time ... my main qualm with Chagnon's attacks against the Salesians was and is that they (the attacks) are consciously false and slanderous. Whether he was legally or illegally in the area is not the center of the discussion."

15. Margolies (1995) writes "Graziano and I were commencing our project on the indigenous architecture of Venezuela and asked Chagnon to collaborate with materials on the Yanomami shabono. We incorporated Chagnon and Hames into our research projects. From 1986-1989, they worked quietly in Venezuela as our collaborators. Chagnon's problems recommenced in 89-90."

16. "Shaki," bee, is Chagnon's nickname among the Yanomami.

17. In fact, no Yanomami has ever killed a European or American. They have more likely been the victims of outside violence and exploitation than its originators.

18. See also John Paul II (1990) in which he speaks of the need for patience in the implementation of the inculturation process. He also warns that inculturation cannot be allowed to threaten what is fundamentally Christian.

19. See Salamone, Nurses, Midwives, and Teachers - Joans-of-All-Trades: The Dominican Sisters in Nigeria. Missiology 5:487-501, 1986.

20. For a discussion of missionary-anthropologist relationships see Salamone 1985 and Whiteman 1985.

21. A recent article about the Jesuit astrophysicist the Reverend George Coyne, S.J., makes an analogous suggestion (Hitt 1994:36-39).

BIBLIOGRAPHY

Albert, Bruce. 1993. "The Massacre of the Yanomami of Hashimu." *Folha de Sao Paulo*. October 10.

_____. 1992. "Indian lands, environmental policy, and military geopolitics in the development of the Brazilian Amazonia: the case of the Yanomami." *Development and Change* 23:34-70.

_____. 1985. *Temps du sang, temps des cendres. Representations de la maladie, system rituel et espace politique chez les Yanomami du Sud-est (Amazonie bresilienne)*. Doctoral Dissertation. Paris: University of Paris X.

Anonymous. 1993. "Death in the Rain Forest." *The New York Times*. August 27: A14.

_____. 1988. "The Violent Yanomami: A New Study Rekindles a Debate over the Roots of Warfare." *Scientific American.* May 3: 17-18

_____. 1988. "Sex and Death in the Jungle." *Discover.* July 10.

Asch, Timothy. 1991. "The Defence of Yanomami Society and Culture: Its Importance and Significance." *La Iglesia en Amazonas* 12 (53):35-38.

Bartholomeusz, D. 1991. T. S. Eliot and "The Golden Bough." *Coll. Anthropol.* 15:339-348.

Beidelman, Thomas O. 1982. *Colonial Evangelism*. Bloomington: Indian University Press.

Blount, Jeb. 1993. "40 Yanomami Indians Slain on Brazilian Reservation." *The Washington Post.* August 21: A17.

Booth, William. 1989. "Warfare over Yanomamo Indians." *Science* March 3: 1138-40.

Bortoli, Jose. 1995. "Transcript of Remarks at the American Anthropological Association Discussion." In Frank A. Salamone, ed. *Who Speaks for the Yanomami? Studies in Third World Societies*. Williamsburg: College of William and Mary.

_____. Interview by Frank A. Salamone. Salesian Mission Stations in the Amazon. November 1994.

_____. 1994. "Los Yanomami y el Parque Parima-Tapirapco." *La Iglesia en Amazonas* 15(65):21-30.

Bower, Bruce. 1991. "Gauging the Winds of War." *Science News.* February 9: 88-90.

Brooke, James. 1993. "Brazilians Reduce Indian Death Toll: Government Says 16, not 73, Were Slain, in Venezuela." *New York Times.* September 1: A4.

_____. 1993. "Attack on Brazilian Indians Is the Worst Since 1910." *New York Times.* August 26: A15.

_____. 1993. "Miners in Brazil Kill 20 Indians in Remote Area." *New York Times.* August 20: A10.

_____. 1992. "Venezuela's Policy for Brazilian Gold Miners: Bulletin." *New York Times.* February 16: 9.

_____. 1991. "Venezuela Befriends Tribe, but What's Venezuela?" *New York Times.* September 11: A8.

_____. 1991. "Crackdowns on Miners Follow Indian Killings." *New York Times.* September 19: Section 1:8.

Bross, Rene. 1988. "El Hombre, Su Fe, Su Cultura, Su Religion." *La Iglesia en Amazonas* 42-43 (December): 89-95.

Bruner, Karen. 1993. "Mystery Deaths in Brazil." *The Christian Science Monitor.* August 31: 6.

Bujo, Benezer. 1992. *African Theology in Its Social Context.* (Translated from the German by John O'Donohue). Naryknoll, NY: Orbis Press.

Burridge, Kenelm. 1991. *In the Way: A Study of Christian Missionary Endeavors.* Vancouver: UBC Press.

Cappelletti, E. J. 1994. "Napoleon A. Chagnon's Column, 'Covering Up the Yanomamo Massacre'." Letter to the Editor. *New York Times.* January 18: A22.

Cardozo, Jesus Ignacio. 1995. E-Mail Response to First-draft of this Manuscript.

Chagnon, Napoleon. 1995. "Transcript of Remarks at the American Anthropological Association Discussion." In Frank A. Salamone, ed. *Who Speaks for the Yanomami? Studies in Third World Societies.* Williamsburg: College of William and Mary.

_____. 1994. "Letter to the Editor." *Interciencia* 19(4):161-162.

_____. 1993. "Covering Up the Yanomamo Massacre." *The New York Times.* October 23:A13.

_____. 1988. "Life Histories, Blood Revenge, and Warfare in a Tribal Population." *Science.* February 26:985-92.

_____. 1968. *Yanomamo: The Fierce People.* New York: Holt,

Cocco, Padre Luis. 1972. *Iyewei-teri:Quince anos entre los Yanomamos.* Caracas: Liberia Editorial Salesiana.

Cockburn, Alexander. 1991. *The Bind That Ties: Missionary Position.* October 14: 434-435.

Colby, Gerard and Charlotte Dennett. 1995. *Thy Will Be Done: The Conquest of the Amazon: Nelson Rockefeller and Evangelism in the Age of Oil*. New York: Harper Collins.

Conway, Jon. 1995. Discussion "Improving Relationships between Anthropologists and Missionaries." Radio Program *On the Mark*, WAVA, Arlington, VA. Guests: Father Jon Conway and Frank A. Salamone, February 2.

Cox, Harvey. 1991. "Inculturation Reconsidered." *Christianity and Crisis* 51: 140-142.

Dimanawe, Cesar. 1990. Letter to Senor Chagnon, reprinted in *La Iglesia en Amazonas* 11(49): 20. Eibl-Eibesfeldt, I and G. Herzog-Schroder.

_____. 1994. "In Defense of Mission." Unpublished manuscript.

_____. 1994. Letter to Bishop Ignacio Velasco. February 28.

Donovan, Vincent J. 1982. *Christianity Rediscovered*. Maryknoll: Orbis Books.

Ferguson, Brian. 1995. "A Reputation for War." *Natural History*. April: 62-63.

_____. 1995. *Yanomami Warfare: A Political History*. Santa Fe: SAR Press.

Finkers, Jan. 1994. "Antwoord Chagnon." *Don Bosco Nu.* 53(5):7-10.

Frazer, James G. 1963. *The Golden Bough*. 1 Volume abridged edition of 1922 2 volume edition. New York: Collier Books.

Good, Kenneth. 1995. "The Yanomami Keep on Trekking." *Natural History*. April:56-61 and 63-65.

_____. 1989. *Yanomami Hunting Patterns: Trekking and Garden Relocation as an Adaptation to Game Availability in Amazonia, Venezuela*. Ph.D. Dissertation. University of Florida.

_____. 1987. "Limiting Factors in Amazonian Ecology." In Marvin Harris and E. Ross, eds. Pp. 407-426. *Food and Evolution: Toward a Theory of Human Food Habits*. Philadelphia: Temple University Press.

Good, Kenneth and David Charnoff. 1991. *Into the Heart One Man's Pursuit of Love and Knowledge Among the Yanomama*. New York: Simon and Schuster.

Harris, Marvin. 1984. "Animal Capture and Yanomami Warfare: Retrospective and New Evidence." *Journal of Anthropological Research* 40: 183-201.

Heffner, Robert W. 1993. "Introduction: World Building and the Rationality of Conversion." Pp. 3-44. In Robert W. Heffner, ed. *Conversion To Christianity: Historical and Anthropological Perspectives on a Great Transformation*. Berkeley: University of California Press.

Hillman, Eugene. 1993. *Toward an African Christianity: Inculturation Applied*. Mahwah, NJ: Paulist Press.

_____. 1989. *Many Paths*. Maryknoll: Orbis Books.

_____. 1975. *Polygamy Reconsidered*. Maryknoll: Orbis Books.

Hitt, Jack. 1994. "Would You Baptize an Extraterrestrial?" *New York Times Magazine*. May 29:36-39.

Horgan, John. 1988. "The Violent Yanomami: A New Study Rekindles a Debate over the Roots of Warfare." *Scientific American* May: 17-19.

Hulme, Peter. 1988. *Colonial Encounters*. New York: Methuen.

Ilogu, Edmund. 1974. "Traditional Ibo Religious Beliefs, Practices and Organizations." Pp. 34-55. In Edmund Ilogu, editor, *Christianity and Ibo Culture*. New York: Nok Publishers.

John Paul II. *Veritatis Splendor*. 1993. Papal Encyclical.

_____. *Redemptoris Missio*. 1990. Papal Encyclical.

Johnson, Paul. 1979. *A History of Christianity*. New York: Atheneum.

Kepp, Michael. 1993. "President of Amazon Gold Miners Says He Will Quit over Massacre." *American Metal Market*. August 26: 4.

Kirwin, Michael. 1988. *The Missionary and the Diviner*. Maryknoll, NY: Orbis Books.

_____. 1988. *How African Traditional Religions Assimilate Christianity*. (Unpub).

_____. 1987. *Anthropology and Divination*. Maryknoll, NY: Orbis Books.

Kopenawa, Davi. Interview. Urihi 16, Bulletin of the CCPY (Comissao pela Criacao do Parque Yanomami). Translated by Bruce Albert. 1993.

Kwyune, David. Interview. The Catholic University of East Africa. January 10, 1991.

Lizot, Jacques. 1985. *Tales of the Yanomami*. Cambridge: Cambridge University Press.

_____. 1984. *Les Yanomami centraux*. Paris: Editions de l'Ecole des Hautes Etudes en Sciences Sociales.

_____. 1976. *Le cercle des feux*. Paris: Editions du Seuil.

_____. 1976. *The Yanomami in the Face of Ethnocide*. Copenhagen: IWGIA.

_____. 1975. *Diccionario Yanomami-Espanol.* Caracas: Universidad Central de Venezuela.

Long, William. 1993. "Amazon Murder Mystery: Yanomamis Say Miners Killed a Clan of Indians." *Los Angeles Times.* August 30: A1.

Luzbetak, Louis J. 1988. *The Church and Cultures.* Maryknoll, NY: Orbis Books.

Malinowski, Bronislaw. 1948. *Magic, Science and Religion.* Boston: Beacon Press.

Marty, Martin. 1987. "Commentary." *Christian Century* 10: 1127.

McDonald, James H. 1993. "Whose History? Whose Voice? Myth and Resistance in the Rise of the New Left in Mexico." *Cultural Anthropology* 8: 96-116.

Mbefo, Luke. 1987. "Theology and Inculturation." *Cross Currents* 37: 393-403.

Ramos, Rita. 1995. *Sanuma Memories: Yanomami Ethnography in Times of Crisis.* Madison: University of Wisconsin Press.

_____. In press. *O papel politica das epidemias. O caso Yanomami. In Grupos Etnicos en Riesgo de Extincion,* ed. M. Bartolome. Quito: Abya-Yala.

_____. 1991. "The Prophecy of a Rumor. The clash between Indians and miners in Yanomamiland." (Unpub.)

_____. 1990. "An Economy of Waste. Amazonian Frontier Development and the Livelihood of Brazilian Indians." Pp. 161-178. In *Economic Catalysts to Ecological Change.* Working Papers, 39th Annual Conference, Center for Latin American Studies, University of Florida, Gainesville.

_____. 1987. "Reflecting on the Yanomami: Ethnographic Images and the Pursuit of the Exotic." *Cultural Anthropology* 2:284-304.

Rinehart & Winston. 1988. Padre Jose Bortoli, San Maria Isabel Eguillor. "Una aplicacion antropologica practica entre los Yanomami: Colaboracion entre misioneros y antropologos." Pp. 42-43. *La Iglesia en Amazonas.* December: 75-83.

Ritchie, Mark Andrew. 1996. *Spirit of the Rainforest: A Yanomamo Shaman's Story.* Chicago: Island Lake Press.

Salamone, Frank A., ed. 1995. *Who Speaks for the Yanomami? Studies in Third World Societies.* Williamsburg: College of William and Mary.

_____. 1994. "Mixed Messages at the Mission, In Laurie Klein and Elizabeth Brusco, eds." Pp. 61-90 in *The Message in the Missionary. Studies in Third World.* Society Press: William and Mary, Williamsburg, VA.

_____. 1991. "Creole Performance and the Mass: The Creolization Process." *Studies in Third World Societies* 46: 21-36.

_____. 1991. "Mixed Messages at the Mission." *Anthropos* 86: 487-499.

_____. 1986. "Joans-Of-All-Trades: The Dominican Sisters in Nigeria." *Missiology* 5:487-501.

_____. 1985. *Missionaries and Anthropologists: Case Studies. Studies in Third World Societies.* Williamsburg, VA.

_____. 1975. "A Continuity of Igbo Values After Conversion: A Study in Purity and Prestige." *Missiology* 3: 33-43.

Schmidt, Wilhelm. 1935. *The Origin and Growth of Religion: Facts and Theories.* Translated by H. J. Rose (Original 1931). London: Metheun.

Serbin, Ken. 1990. "Amazon Gold Prospectors a Threat to Yanomami Indians." *National Catholic Reporter.* February 23: 7.

Smole, William J. 1976. *The Yanomama Indians: A Cultural Geography.* Austin: University of Texas Press.

Sponsel, Leslie, ed. 1996. *Indigenous Peoples and the Future of Amazonia.* Phoenix: University of Arizona Press.

Taylor, Kenneth I. 1981. "Knowledge and Praxis in Sanuma Food Prohibitions." Pp. 24-54. In K. Kensinger and W. Kracke, eds. *Food Taboos in Lowland South America.* Working Papers on South American Indians 3. Bennington College.

_____. 1977. *Raiding, Dueling, and Descent Group Membership Among the Sanuma. Actes du XLIIe Congres International des Americanistes 2: 91-104.* Paris: Societe des Americanistes.

_____. 1976. "Body and Spirit among the Sanuma (Yanomama) of North Brazil." In F. X. Grollig and H.B. Haley, eds. *Medical Anthropology.* The Hague: Mouton.

_____. 1974. *Sanuma Fauna Prohibitions and Classifications. Monograph 18.* Caracas: Fundacion La Salle de Ciencias Naturales.

Turner, Terence. 1993. "Brazil's Guilt in the Amazon Massacre." *New York Times.* August 26: A21.

_____. 1991. *Uno grupos de Missionaros del Alto Orinoco. Consideraciones a un Documento de Charles Brewer Carias.* Pamphlet.

Vatican II. *The Decree on the Church's Missionary Activity.* December 7, 1965. Ad Gentes.

_____. *Gaudium et Spes, No. 58.* 1965.

van der Geest, Sjaak and Jon P. Kirby. 1992. "The Absence of the Missionary in African Ethnography, 1930-1965." *African Studies Review* 35: 59-103.

Vicente, Josefa. 1988. "La Situacion Indigena: Punto de convergencia entre Antropologos y Mioneros. Entrevita al Doctor Napoleon Chagnon." *La Iglesia en Amazonas* 42-43 (December):85-88.

Vista, Boa. 1993. "Brazil Miners Grouse in Wake of Massacre." *American Metal Market.* October 20: 5.

Weinberg, Bill. 1996. "For God (and the C.I.A.)." *Nation* 26(9): 29-32.

Whiteman, Darrel. 1985. *Anthropologists and Missionaries - I.* Williamsburg, VA: Studies in Third World Societies.

Winkler, Karen. 1994. "Bitter Warfare in Anthropology." *Chronicle of Higher Education.* October 26: A10, A18-119.

Winokur, L. A. 1993. "Emissary from the Rain Forest." *The Progressive.* March 19: 14.

INDEX

About the Author

Frank A. Salamone (Ph.D. SUNY-Buffalo, 1973) is a full professor of anthropology and sociology at Iona College, New Rochelle, New York. He has conducted research in Nigeria, Kenya, Ghana, Venezuela and the United States. His interests have been religion and identity. After many years studying other people's religion and identity, he decided to study that of his own ethnic group in his own home town, Rochester, New York. He has published extensively on Italian Americans in Rochester, New York and is planning to publish a history of that group up to the end of World War II. He was born in Rochester, New York in 1939. He is married and he and his wife, Virginia, have two children, a boy and a girl. He received a BA in history from St. John Fisher College, an MA in history from the University of Rochester, and a Ph.D. in anthropology from SUNY-Buffalo.

About the Contributors

Dr. Teodoro Marcano has worked with both Napoleon Chagnon and Padre Jose Bortoli. He has great respect for both men and their work. He has stated that he does not believe the Salesians are harming the Yanomami and that they are aware of the nutritional needs of the Indians. By the same token, he is a supporter of Chagnon's efforts to aid their survival in the modern world. He was pleased to be part of the effort to solve the dispute between the Salesians and Chagnon and bring the discussion back to the problems of the Yanomami where it belongs.

Padre Jose Bortoli is an Italian Salesian born in Padua, the adopted home of the Portuguese saint beloved of Italians, Anthony of Padua. Bortoli has spent most of his life in Venezuela, over 25 years on the Orinoco. He speaks Yanomami fluently, has worked with anthropologists and doctors to understand their perspectives and in order to help the Yanomami. He states that he has made no converts in all his years of missionary work. Moreover, his work is not about making converts but about bearing witness. Bortoli feels kindly toward Chagnon and regrets the harm the dispute has done the Yanomami and the cause of scientific and spiritual cooperation. He sees no essential conflict between missionaries and anthropologists, both of whom should strive to serve the people involved.

Greg Sanford is a missionary representative for the New Tribes Missions. He has spent many years as a missionary in Venezuela and travels there frequently on mission business.

The Yanomami are eager to have their opinions known. There is no single person who speaks for all Yanomami. In fact, the idea of Yanomami unity is a new idea to them but one that will become increasingly important as they take their rightful place in Venezuelan and Brazilian society. Meanwhile, individual Yanomami are willing to speak to those who are willing to listen. On major issues there is basic agreement about safeguarding their way of life. There are disagreements on particular issues just as there are among any people. But on the issue of who rightfully speaks for the Yanomami there is no disagreement. The Yanomami speak for themselves.

Water damaged / stains

DATE DUE front
cover
pin
9/8/08

OCT 0 9 1998		
	JUN 0 1 2007	
SEP 1 6 1998	UIC OCT 0 7 2008	
MAR 1 0 1999	Rec'd OCT 2 1 2008	
JUN 0 7 2000		
JUN 0 1 2000		
JUN 0 7 2001		
JAN 0 7 2001		
DEC 0 3 2002		
FEB 1 8 2005		
MAY 1 8 2005		

Demco, Inc. 38-293